A Tiger Remembers

A Tiger Remembers
The Way We Were
in Singapore

Ann Wee

RIDGE BOOKS
SINGAPORE

© 2017 Ann Wee

Published under the Ridge Books imprint by:

NUS Press
National University of Singapore
AS3-01-02, 3 Arts Link
Singapore 117569

Fax: (65) 6774-0652
E-mail: nusbooks@nus.edu.sg
Website: http://nuspress.nus.edu.sg

ISBN: 978-981-4722-37-7 (paper)

National Library Board, Singapore Cataloguing-in-Publication Data

Name(s): Wee, Ann
Title: A tiger remembers: the way we were in Singapore / Ann Wee.
Description: Singapore: Ridge Books, 2017. | Includes bibliographical references.
Identifier(s): OCN 954009232 | ISBN 978-981-47-2237-7 (paperback)
Subject(s): LCSH: Singapore -- Anecdotes. | Singapore -- Social conditions
        -- 20th century -- Anecdotes.
Classification: DDC 959.5705--dc23

Typeset by: Pressbooks.com
Printed by: Mainland Press Pte Ltd

To the family in all its 101 different shapes and sizes.
With its capacity to cope which ranges from truly
marvellous to distinctly tatty: still, in one form
or another, the best place for most of us to be.

When you meet another man's culture,
Take off your shoes.
Lest you tread on another man's dream.

—Max Warren (1964)

Contents

Acknowledgements   xi

Foreword   xv

Introduction: Why this is a Memoir and Not a Work of Fiction   xix

PART I. A BIT ON THE PERSONAL SIDE: CULTURE LEARNING NEAR THE OLD HOME

1. Tigerishness   3

2. Tiger at Downton Abbey!: A Teenage Experience "at the Coal Face"   7

3. "Problem of the Aged"?   15

4. An Assortment of Small Graves   19

PART II. MAINLY SINGAPORE: CULTURE LEARNING IN A NEW HOME

5. A Life Journey, with this and that Picked Up along the Way   27

6. Glimpses of World War II: One Man Moves On from a Massacre   41

CONTENTS

7. Children and Childhood in the Singapore   45
   Chinese Family: An Experience of Culture
   Learning

8. The Early Days of the Singapore Family   54

9. The Low-income Family Arrives: Singapore   61
   Housing before the HDB "Revolution"

10. The Singleton Dormitory: Constructing a   72
   Social System in the Absence of Family

11. Loos and Related Topics   80

12. Names: Fifty Shades of Getting Messed Around   87

13. Adoption: Some Highways and Byways   93

14. Ambushed by the Indian National Army   103

15. A Vignette of Violence   110

16. A Funeral in the Tan Family   114

17. A Short Meditation on the Subject of Wisdom   118

   Conclusion   123
   Bibliography   126

Acknowledgements

A patchwork such as this, by its very nature, means difficulties in managing to acknowledge all who have, in some way or another, contributed to its make-up. But one has to start somewhere.

I should start with my parents, from whom I learned at an early age that life can be more interesting if you venture across cultural boundaries. I must be one of the very few middle-class English children of my generation who ever spent a morning sitting in a Romany caravan. Several Romany families used regularly to rest their horses for a few days in a field near our house, on their way to an annual fair. They were regarded, by most in the neighbourhood, with perhaps some trepidation and even disdain, but my father was soon leaning over the field gate, engaging the men in conversation. He also gave them fresh vegetables from the surplus which our garden regularly produced.

Arising from these conversations, on one occasion I was lifted bodily into one of the caravans and seated, drinking overly sweet tea in the welcome warmth of the cast-iron stove, which was a rather surprising feature of the interior. There was a gleaming cleanliness about that interior, from the lino-covered floor to the shining brass fittings all about. The tea was a wildly unsuitable drink for a child of my age—four or perhaps five—which added to the sense of adventure. And it was rather nice being treated as an exotic doll by the smiling, long-skirted women in black shawls.

Afterwards, my mother was a bit concerned about that tea but clearly no harm was done and she was soon eagerly listening to the details of my cross-cultural venture, which I was equally eager to relate. Thanks, Mum and Dad!

And in adult life I must pay tribute to my accommodating and kindly in-laws and to my spouse, all of whom helped to provide a "soft landing" when I crossed cultural boundaries from West to East. They combined to make it all so much easier than others had predicted it would be!

For my first six months in Singapore I gained greatly from the mentorship, on matters cultural, by my senior London School of Economics classmate, the late Maurice Freedman, who was just finishing the two years of Singapore fieldwork on which his great 1957 monograph is based.

It is a pleasure and a privilege to put on record my own debt and tribute to the contribution to local knowledge, deriving from the research undertaken by the mature-age students who enrolled in the Diploma in Social Studies course. This course was offered by the University of Malaya and then (from 1960), the University of Singapore, between 1952 and 1974. A third of the diploma's second (and final) year's work comprised an individual research project.

Prior to the onset of the diploma course, there had been very little published in social research. Until 1967 there was no Sociology Department in the university, and initially the Social Welfare Department's 1947 Social Survey was almost the only publication other than the censuses of population. Moreover, it was still some years before oral history became a legitimate field for the historian.

The rich store of ethnographies which arose from the diploma research covers many aspects of the life of those times: village studies, minority communities, single immigrant dormitories, "backyard" industries, experiences of early HDB rehousing, health practices and much else. I learned a very great deal from my association with the diploma cohort—those cited in the Bibliography represent only a small fraction of the whole.

ACKNOWLEDGEMENTS

Much to the credit of the diploma students, their research work caught the attention of the eminent scholars G. William Skinner and Maurice Freedman, who sought copies of this work for the libraries of Cornell and LSE respectively. Much knowledge of Singapore's social warp and weft, in the days before modernisation, would have been lost forever but for this treasure of ethnographic studies.

All through my sixty-seven years in Singapore, I have been privileged to encounter interesting people who enriched my culture learning. I have warm initial memories of the Methodist Girls' School teachers, who welcomed me into their midst in late 1950. From the interactions at staffroom coffee times, I learned so much of Peranakan family systems and values (and patois!), which greatly enhanced my settling in as a member of the Singapore English-educated middle class. Then, in 1955–6, as staff of the then Social Welfare Department on old Havelock Road, I encountered, and learned from, a whole different level of local life.

In my many years of association with the university, I have enjoyed learning from colleagues and students, along with the pleasures of friendship. Students graduated to become field colleagues, who brought their enriching experience to meetings of various levels and settings. It has been an enjoyable privilege to gain from ongoing contact with them and their professional situations.

To the people whose naming misadventures I have described in Chapter 12, I apologise that I was unable to consult you at the point of publication, and I must just hope that you share my belief that these misadventures should go down on record.

Thanks to named individuals must start with acknowledging the invaluable help of Dr Mandakini Arora, without whose warm encouragement and assistance this venture might never have got off the ground. Her interest in the topics and her impeccable command of English made her the perfect coach urging on from the sidelines and providing a preliminary editor role. Dr Arora's sister, professional editor Mrs Sunandini Arora Lal, also gave her generous assistance. The friendship of this scholarly and delightful family has been an added bonus.

To Mr Janadas Devan, Director, Institute of Policy Studies and Chief of Government Communications, I am deeply indebted for his generous willingness to write the Foreword for this volume. In view of the many calls on his time, I hope this was a chore that he felt he could dash off while having breakfast!

At NUS Press, the willingness of Dr Paul Kratoska and Mr Peter Schoppert to show interest in this manuscript was a delightful surprise, for which I am truly grateful. I had assumed that a manuscript which includes the bells and whistles of a style intended to appeal to a readership of upper secondary education, would fall below their radar screen. And all praise is due to the patience of Dr Pallavi Narayan, who cheerfully tolerated my Neanderthal inability to cope with editing in soft copy.

Foreword

.

"Experience is not what happens to a man," Aldous Huxley wrote once, "it is what a man does with what happens to him."

The same might be said of a life—in particular, the life of the indomitable and incomparable Ann Wee. A life is not a record of what happens to a woman; a life is what that woman does with what happens to her: what she does to shape what happens to her into significant form; what she does to infuse the boom and buzz—the ceaseless tick-tock—of existence with meaning.

One can't imagine Mrs Wee saying of herself, as Christopher Isherwood—another writer that she would have come across as she came of age in the England of the 1940s—did of himself: "I am a camera with its shutter open, quite passive, recording, not thinking."

Passive—not actively seizing? Ann? Merely recording—not grasping, catching, snatching at every stray experience as it slips by? Not thinking? Ann?

No, not Ann. Not Ann when she was a mere four- or five-year-old sitting in a Romany caravan, sipping "overly-sweet tea". Not the eighteen-year-old Ann, serving as a maid in a Red Cross hospital in the final years of World War II: scrubbing floors, skinning rabbits, and sleeping in a dorm full of coalminers' daughters. Not the twenty-three-year-old Ann, sailing to Singapore in the economy class of a ship to be reunited with her Singaporean fiancée, H.L. Wee, whom she was to marry soon after at St Andrew's Cathedral. Not the Mrs Ann Wee who first taught at Methodist Girls' School, served in the colonial Social Welfare Department then taught at the University of Singapore. Not the Professor Ann Wee who never fails to bob up from her seat at every conference, workshop, seminar, talk that I've seen her at over the last three decades, to ask just the right question, make the apt remark, recall a hilarious incident or disclose a fascinating insight.

Take, for instance, what she says here of the slums of Chinatown that she first visited as a social work educator in the Singapore of the 1950s: "The emergence of a mass of low-income families in the 1920s and 1930s set a trend for Singapore to represent some of the most grossly overcrowded slum conditions in the world. But from the lifestyle of those I visited I estimate these were slums of hope. Charles J. Stokes draws a distinction between what he calls 'slums of hope' and 'slums of despair'. As a student volunteer in the poorest parts of London in the 1940s, I had visited homes where the living conditions were indescribably squalid. On returning home after a visit, it was necessary to stand in the long bath and change clothes to the skin, lest one had brought home fleas or other forms of vermin. Britain had had compulsory education since 1870, and the slum population that I encountered in the 1940s had, for some reason, failed, for several generations, to get their feet onto the running board of upward mobility. These were slums of despair. In contrast, the people of the slums in Singapore had never had much in the way of a chance in life, and as Singapore developed they were ready to use every opportunity to move on and up to a better general standard of living. The personal histories of many older leaders in the public and private sectors illustrates this lifetime trajectory."

This is only one example of what the reader might find in this volume. One wouldn't find here the usual fare of a personal memoir. There is very little of what Ann or Mrs Wee or Professor

Wee—"the founding mother of social work in Singapore", she has been called—might have felt, subjectively, at any point in her life. Instead, there is much of what the author at different stages of her career observed, reflected upon, absorbed and stitched together into a pattern. And that pattern is not external to Mrs Wee, constituting a reality apart from her; Mrs Wee *is* the pattern that she makes of her observations. A life is not a record of what happens to a woman; a life is what that woman does with what happens to her.

This is truly the memoir of a social anthropologist; a social observer with a very fine and intricately intuitive grasp of human beings as they relate to each other; someone who dedicated herself to the study and teaching of social work primarily because she habitually saw people as social beings. I don't mean to suggest by that anything fussy or academic in her impulses and perceptions (if anything, she is always wonderfully refreshing and direct). I only mean to observe that Mrs Wee's primary lens of looking at the world is social. Just as some people habitually look at life or society historically or politically, Mrs Wee habitually looks at individuals or life in their social aspects: men and women, young or old, manual labourers or mothers-in-law, as they exist in a group; the meaning of any one individual or event to be found thus not in their singularity but by virtue of their relationship to a vast number of other individuals or events. Thinking socially seems to come to her as naturally as thinking historically comes to me or thinking musically might come to a composer. The reader can take a look at the fascinating chapter on loos or the chapter on a funeral or the delightful one on names to get a flavour of what I mean. That is why I found so much in this book fascinating—from her meditation on "child training" in Chinese families to midwifery to newspaper obituaries.

One last thing I should note: Mrs Wee is a Singaporean, but don't expect her to resemble any Singaporean you might be familiar with. Being a Singaporean is not a matter of birth or ancestry, as the late S. Rajaratnam once observed, it is a matter of conviction and choice. Mrs Wee is living proof of that dictum. She is still very English—her accent so undimmed by the decades of separation from England, her birthplace, that she still pronounces the "o" in "petrol" like a bell—yet she is undeniably Singaporean.

Like "us" but herself. "Foreign" yet familiar. Born overseas but "Made in Singapore".

Mrs Ann Wee is *sui generis*.

Introduction: Why this is a Memoir and Not a Work of Fiction

"Unlike in the case of poor Sleeping Beauty, the bad fairy stayed away from my baptism. But that bitch-kitty sure did make up for lost time on the day of my wedding."

For a while I had the illusion that this would make a great opening sentence for a fine work of fiction, AW's great first novel! Some pundit has stated that there is a novel inside everyone. Well, he got it wrong; inside me there is no novel. That may be a pretty good opening sentence, but at that point I dried up as a creative writer.

But I wander off-track: too much about what this volume is *not*, whereas an Introduction must focus on what the reader can anticipate in the pages to come. I have no novel to present, but I very much hope that I can interest you, instead, in a book of memoirs and reminiscences. Perhaps to compensate for my total incapacity as a creative writer, I have been gifted with recall of many details which are highly unlikely to feature in any formal book of history. A major (but not sole) object of putting the various items together herein is to get on record some highways, but mostly byways, of the past in Singapore.

In addition to Singapore stories, I have added a few personal thoughts and early personal recollections which I hope you, the reader, will find interesting. For example, Singapore friends have been talking about the television series based on the British "upstairs–downstairs" television serial *Downton Abbey*. These include episodes in which, during wartime, that noble mansion became a military hospital. While still a teenager living in England in wartime 1944, I had the rather unusual experience of working as a live-in domestic servant in just such a stately-home-becomes-military-hospital. I have risked including this adventure, and indeed my hospital was just as ridden with eyebrow-raising social class distinctions as is Downton Abbey of the television series. I hope that an account of all this may prove to be entertaining.

My personal hospital working experience, moreover, contains a lesson which may be of relevance to Singapore and, indeed, in general. As I discovered, one does not have to move far from home to experience culture learning. Sharing a dormitory with girls who were, like me, English, but who had grown up in a poor coalmining town, exposed me, middle-class AW, to what amounted to culture shock. We all need, even in our own societies, to move out of our comfort zone and encounter those whose cultures, be it in ethnicity or in socio-economic status, are different from our own. Singapore men may experience this in National Service, but culture learning is enriching for us all.

You will notice that in the Contents are two chapters (3 and 4) which appear to dwell on old age and death. I can assure you that these, in fact, represent a call to celebrate life. It is so easy in this era to take longevity for granted, and instead to focus on problems of provision for the aged. These problems are indeed very real, and major developments in our social policies must be set in place to tackle this coming pattern of Singapore demography. But what we can too easily forget is the fantastic privilege of life expectancy that we enjoy. Barring some fairly rare misfortune, we can look forward to being part of the living world until our late seventies or eighties. Not everyone enjoys a good old age, but the present situation is a decided improvement on the experience of our ancestors. For them, surviving even babyhood was a not-to-be-taken-for-granted achievement. Indeed, it is hard to envisage how our ancestors coped emotionally with the perpetual presence of death in the family circle. Nor were only the poor victims of this general fragility of life; even others, like the pioneering Sir Stamford Raffles, managed to rear only one child out of five born to him, and that one surviving daughter died aged nineteen.

The chapters which are about Singapore represent my own (second) experience of culture learning, which began with my first arrival by ship in early 1950. There is much in every culture which only the insider fully understands, but there are also factors which the insider takes for granted and never thinks about but of which the outsider is uniquely conscious. For example, in Chapter 5, I mention the way my Singapore friends always spoke of their siblings. Their references to "my second sister" and "my third brother" represented a taken-for-granted consciousness of family as a structure, quite different from the individualistic "my sister Mary" and "my brother Tom" sibling referrals to which I was accustomed in England.

The two chapters on the early family in Singapore and on the living arrangements of those who came without a family, are really two sides of the same phenomenon. Early Singapore was far from being a normal society; it was more like a long-stay central business district or CBD. The vast majority of the population, at least up to the 1920s, comprised (mainly) men who came with a plan to earn more than they could in their home country, and then to return to their home country and settle back into family life as prosperous residents. The largest number came from China and India, but many came also from what are now Malaysia and Indonesia.

Less recognised is the fact that this same career pattern, though less openly articulated, applied to the British colonial administrators and business people. With very few exceptions, the British returned to their home country on retirement, having enjoyed, in Singapore, a career more rewarding than if they had worked in Britain. This was quite a different "game plan" from British migration to, say, Australia, Canada or New Zealand, to which countries people migrated with the intention of settling on a permanent basis.

This "CBD mentality" perhaps explains why there was so little interest in becoming independent from Britain until after the harrowing experience of Japanese occupation (1942–5). From 1945 onwards, independence for Singapore became a major political issue. In the 1930s, the Singapore Chinese were passionately active in work to support the preservation of the independence of China from Japan. In 1943, Singapore Indians became active in a fight for the independence of India from Britain. As long as Pax Britannica and free-trade policies made Singapore a great CBD for those who came to work and earn, colonialism was not seen as much of a problem.

World War II changed everything; the British seemed to crumble all too easily in the face of Japanese invasion. In his memoirs, Mr Lee Kuan Yew recalls as a very young man, hearing the sound of the explosion by which the British blew up the Singapore–Johor causeway, in a vain effort to halt the Japanese onslaught. He recalls saying to himself that the explosion was the sound of the British Empire going up in smoke. Indeed, the experience of the fall of Singapore made Pax Britannica seem like an unreliable myth.

In relation to the World War II era in Singapore, I have ventured to include a chapter on the Indian National Army, an amazing phenomenon that should be regarded as part of the history of India, though largely arising and choreographed in Singapore. It is one of the odd quirks of history that not only the British but also the Government of India itself have preferred to airbrush this whole episode out of national memory. I have chosen to cover this topic in a style which is almost a review article in praise of an outstandingly readable book. I am well aware that it is an episode in our history about which very few Singaporeans have knowledge or indeed great interest. My hope is that this chapter will arouse more curiosity about the subject and that some readers will then follow up with further reading on their own.

Just imagine—locally recruited young Singapore Indian women soldiers as well as men! More than 500 young women in uniform were camped in what had been the playing fields of St Joseph's Institution on Bras Basah Road. They could be seen daily marching out in military order, and becoming skilled in hand grenade and bayonet warfare. All part of the history of our peace-loving Singapore!

Chapter 15 describes one afternoon in the early 1950s when the Singapore streets were far from being the abode of peace, something that today we tend to regard as a "Singapore human right". Perhaps this will serve as a reminder that peaceful streets are indeed a precious privilege, which it is unwise to take for granted as we so easily tend to do.

I make no apology for the fact that the reader may occasionally need to consult a dictionary. I too frequently need to enhance my own reading by looking up the meaning of some word with which I am not familiar. I regard this as a normal aspect of lifelong learning. I have checked any word or phrase that I anticipate may be unfamiliar against the 1998 edition of the *New Oxford Dictionary of English*. The twenty-first-century reader will have access to even more sophisticated resource options.

The great British orchestral conductor of an earlier age, Sir Thomas Beecham, claimed to have a personal list of short, entertaining pieces of music with which he liked to end a concert, to send his audience home in a smiling mood. He called this collection "my lollipops". I hope that Chapter 17 of this volume will fall more or less into an equivalent "lollipop" category. Wisdom may sound like a somewhat serious topic, but it can also be looked at from some lighter (though less serious) angles, especially when the practice and understanding of wisdom pops up and hits you from an unexpected source.

A 2014 publication of the Folio Society includes a chapter on writing an introduction. According to this article, "Above everything else, an introduction must express convincing and knowledgeable enthusiasm" on the part of the writer. Really? Surely the most that the writer can hope for is that the reader will experience that enthusiasm, and will judge that the writer was indeed knowledgeable. As the lawyer says in court, "I rest my case."

PART 1

A Bit on the Personal Side: Culture Learning Near the Old Home

Tigerishness

Yes reader, you are, of course, quite correct, there is no such English word as "tigerishness", and I have just made it up. But then it refers to something totally alien to the English concept of "tiger", namely one jungle animal of the cat family, full stop.

Tigerishness is a quality deeply embedded in the Chinese horoscope culture, that sees time as divided into cycles of twelve animal years (Lip 1981 provides interesting material on Chinese horoscopes). Each of these animal years confers some horoscopic characteristics on babies born in that year. Most years confer something favourable on boys or girls, though there is some variation. The most horoscopically blessed of all babies are those born in the Year of the Dragon.

For a girl, there is one year that is fine for her brother but disastrous for her, namely the Year of the Tiger. The Tiger girl was believed to "eat" her husband, and be generally bad for her in-laws. In the past the parents of a Tiger girl faced great difficulties in arranging her marriage.

In relation to this difficulty, we have some quite hard data. The late Dr Tye Cho-Yook, a distinguished demographer formerly in the medical faculty of the now National University of Singapore, made a rather piquant discovery. While we had no general hard data on the age at marriage until 1961 and the passing into law of the Women's Charter, registration of Singapore births had been a legal requirement from as far back as the nineteenth century. And the details of registration included the age of the mother at the time of the birth. While not all babies got registered, this meant we did have a good deal of information going way back, on the age of the mother at the birth of her first baby, which Dr Tye calculated would be, on average, about one year after marriage.

Dr Tye's data showed that every eleventh and thirteenth year there were more than average numbers of women, with markedly fewer than average numbers of women every twelfth year. From this he drew the only possible Singapore conclusion, namely that the family of a young Tiger woman was lying about the daughter's age. That is, in order to get her married, they were claiming she was either one year younger or one year older than she really was. They were "advertising" her as either a nice, domesticated and old-fashioned Ox or as a peace-loving and friendly Rabbit, and concealing the fact that she was, in fact, a much-feared Tiger girl.

Only very recently have parents had the truly abominable option of aborting a foetus that was not the sex they preferred. Moreover, infanticide was never a tolerated practice in a British colony. Therefore, what Dr Tye inferred is the only possible interpretation of the odd age distribution pattern of his data. Unfortunately, Dr Tye never published his findings on the Tiger year.

The earliest of my many indiscretions was to be born in the Year of the Tiger. The twelve-year animal cycle exists within a larger sixty-year "element" cycle—of Wood, Gold, Water, Fire and Earth. I had to make things worse—by being born in 1926, the Year of the Fire Tiger. And my hour of birth was in the middle of the night, which is regarded as even more sinister. In terms of my horoscope, with regard to date, year and time of birth, I hit rock-bottom.

By every possible mystical indicator, I was totally unsuitable for

4

marriage into a Chinese family. Blessedly, a good fairy presided over my marriage and provided me with a Chinese mother-in-law who, though born in Hong Kong, had grown up in the colony of British Guiana (BG) (now Guyana) on mainland South America. The BG Chinese were all baptised Christians and, being a small minority community in that country, had become, within a generation, monolingual English speakers. They retained many Chinese values, strong family ties and skills in entrepreneurship, for example, but lost a lot of cultural details. My dear and warmly remembered mother-in-law was completely "horoscopically challenged". Greatly to my benefit, she didn't know a Rabbit from a Horse. She knew nothing of the significance of "tigerishness". Eventually two of her daughters-in-law, both quite close to her, were Tiger women, without, fortunately, either of us bringing any of the threatened disasters on the clan.

This was all largely the culture of the past, but it took some time to die away. I recall when working in the 1960s with the adoption sub-committee of the Singapore Children's Society, we watched to see what would happen when the Year of the Tiger came around. Happily, we did not have one instance where a baby girl was being given away because she was a Tiger. In several instances the birth parents did refer to her being a Tiger baby, but in every case there was some other circumstance that would most probably have led to the baby's being given away in any year. For example, the family already had had too many baby girls or a mother too weak with TB to cope with another child.

The sub-committee did, however, have some difficulties in placing the baby girls born that year. I recall a couple who took a great fancy to one baby. They assured us that, as they were Christians, horoscopic beliefs had no meaning for them. The next day, they returned to cancel the arrangement. The husband's aunt had been adamant that it was unwise to take such a risk. We had no way of knowing if this was truly a case of an all-powerful aunt or whether it was the couple who had "developed cold feet" and the aunt provided a convenient cover for beliefs to which, as Christians, they would have found it embarrassing to admit.

At the time of writing, the most recent Year of the Tiger was 2010. Happily, I do not recall hearing any concern expressed about babies born in that year. Let us hope that that noble beast the tiger has sloughed off his unfortunate horoscopic shenanigans, and ambled elegantly back to the jungle and grasslands where he most properly belongs.

2

Tiger at Downton Abbey!: A Teenage Experience "at the Coal Face"

Many viewers have watched the serial drama *Downton Abbey* either on television or video. In that story, during wartime the noble family withdrew to live in a wing of the Abbey, while the mansion's main rooms became a military hospital to accommodate soldiers recovering from battle wounds. During World War II this was true of many of England's "stately homes", including Howick Hall, Northumberland, where a Tiger worked as a teenage volunteer.

In the summer of 1944, soon after the "D-Day" invasion, when Allied troops re-invaded mainland Europe, the present elderly titled owner of Howick Hall was still a small boy. He was scampering round the gardens of the wing of the house retained for the noble family's use, while a middle-class eighteen-year-old Red Cross volunteer was down on her knees, scrubbing the floors of the great main building entrance hall and learning the finer points of the English system of social status and class.

The nursing staff of this temporary military hospital had paid leave, but there was no such arrangement for the maids who scrubbed floors and tended to the kitchens. Only if the county Junior Red Cross (JRC) clubs could rustle up live-in volunteers could maids get time off without loss of the wages much needed by their families.

At that time I had completed my A-levels and was free until university term started. While the JRC did not have much success in this recruitment drive, my mildly socialist parents thought this was an excellent opportunity for me to do something useful and to get me out of my middle-class "comfort zone", to learn something of how other people lived. My subsequent experience confirmed that they were thinking along the right lines.

The entrance-hall scrubbing, referred to above, started at 6.30 am, just inside the stately plate-glass double front doors: three of us from "house", sloshing along side by side, edging our knees awkwardly backwards along what seemed like a mile in length. One bumbling JRC volunteer wedged between two "house" professionals of roughly the same age, daughters of pitmen from a coalmining town 20 miles away. Their pace winded the volunteer but they managed to scrub efficiently, natter and giggle all at the same time. Perhaps I was given the middle strip because it was the most trodden on and troublesome to clean. If so, it was a small matter. I was scrubbing for a few weeks before going to university; for the other two, floors to be scrubbed stretched into the future as far as the eye could see.

By the time we scrubbers completed the hall, "house" and "kitchens" were gathering in the servants' dining room. With not even a cup of tea before the scrubbing marathon, the 8.30 am breakfast glowed as a food fest. Viewed more objectively, it was stodgy and positively squelching with saturates—tombstones of the rather heavy wartime bread, fried in beef dripping and topped with "reconstituted" scrambled egg (dried egg powder being all most people had in wartime).

This food was accompanied by tea so strong that, before adding milk, it shimmered almost purple, like the iridescent colours of a starling's wing. For me, a quarter cup topped up with water became marginally drinkable. But "drowning good tea" was a breach of the dining-room code. My daily trips round to the kettle were always accompanied by jeers at my lily-livered failure to appreciate the good things of life. "Real people" drank "real tea", strong enough to float a horseshoe: "some people" seemed to prefer "dishwater". In everything else they were friendly and accepting, but a good deal of passive aggression was worked off over the issue of tea.

Only of breakfast do I recall much in the way of culinary detail, but meals were memorable occasions of which food was only one item. The rather elderly and soft-spoken lady's maid from "the Wing" presided at the head of table. She wore a flowered rayon smock while the rest of us wore starched white gear, including white caps, the details of which varied with the status of the wearer. I was given a whispered warning that the lady's maid was sent over by "the family" to spy on us. If so, she was something of a double agent, regaling us generously with fascinating (though hardly inflammatory) details of life in "the Wing". The other main speaker was the head housemaid—stern, scrawny, middle-aged and rather sharp-tongued—blessedly removed by several layers of authority from the scrubbing team. I recall listening with fascination as she related with indignant triumph how someone had assumed her family's house would have a street number whereas it had, in fact, a name. This was my first intimation of a gaping social void between "Number 19" and "Rose Cottage". I was intrigued. Disappointingly, my parents hooted with laughter when I later sought to enlighten them on this nice social distinction.

Meals were a welcome break in a long working day. One either knocked off at 6 pm or took a three-hour afternoon break and worked the 6–9 pm shift. I recall that evening work was light, more a case of being there if needed. It was during this relaxed time that the rather fearsome head housemaid showed me, as a special favour, some of the magnificent rooms (unused by the family in wartime) of which she, impeccable in her professional duties, was the trusted keeper. For an eighteen-year-old, my first exposure to 20-foot-high, beautifully decorated ceilings, and walls lined with cherry-patterned red silk was an awesome experience.

My arrival must have been a trial for this worthy but formidable woman. Although some 70 or 80 miles from the location of the noble house, by unfortunate coincidence, her family and mine lived in the same village. In that village she had let it be known that her work status was "housekeeper". She was indeed a valued employee but her wearing starched uniform and cap labelled her very clearly a "head housemaid", a position much less august than "housekeeper". On returning home, with rather "bitchy" teenage glee I regaled my parents with this distinctly juicy information. In return I received a very stern parental sermon. Should I breathe so much as a murmur of this in the village, I would become an immediate candidate for one of the less attractive lower levels of Dante's *Inferno*. It was absolutely none of my business!

Soon after 9 pm, "house" scrubbers and junior members of "kitchen" retired to a quite pleasant dormitory up in the attic floor of the house. Bedtime routine was a cultural eye-opener: uniforms came off but everything else remained in situ except for the weekly bath night. There was no heating in the attic, and on recovering from my utter shock at this unheard of habit, I could see that in winter there must have been good, practical reasons for this retention of all but the top layer. This practice should have resulted in raging "b.o." (body odour), but I do not recall that this was so. By that date the civilising influence of Odorono had colonised the grammar schools: perhaps the lower-level secondary schools had also been pheromonally tamed by then.

Shock number two was that hairbrushes and combs were cleaned promiscuously out of the window, with scant respect for the splendid lawns and noble sweep of gravel driveway below. Generations of mining town-bred hair, drifting down silently in the night, must, over decades, have contributed to the organic composition of the soil—or perhaps clogged up the drains.

In the dormitory culture there was an oral myth disparaging bedroom modesty: "Nothing you've got that I haven't got." But behaviour, in practice, was modest in the extreme. However, when the lights were out, chatter ventured in directions it never took in "clear and brightsome day". With much muffled giggling, matrilineally acquired wisdom emerged on a range of intimate topics, decreeing, for example, that husbands were to be valued in the inverse ratio of their virility. Ranging into scatological territory, great sympathy was expressed for an older and well-liked member of the "house" team who suffered from some mysterious bowel complaint. The vocabulary and innuendoes of this complaint's excruciating details were way beyond the outsider's range, but it seemed indelicate to enquire. Besides, any evidence of naivety was pounced on with discomfiting glee.

In view of the diet, no bowel complaint would have been surprising. For example, not once do I recall fruit being served. Beautiful baskets of seasonal fruit were delivered from various gentry households in the neighbourhood but these were always earmarked "for the nurses", a discrimination which seemed to be accepted without question and was never commented upon. As in the case of leave with pay, the domestic staff were invisible.

When my counterpart on "house" returned from her break, someone else took time off and I was transferred to take her duties in the kitchens—and maintain a quite different relationship with hospital life. The "house" staff passed nurses and pyjama-clad patients on brisk errands, but were mostly detached from "hospital" where chores were carried out by patient-orderlies. In corridors we had occasional reminders of what "hospital" was all about. We were instructed to smile and not look shocked when heavily bandaged figures shoulder-nudged through swing doors, face, head and arms totally swathed, eyes always seeming unnaturally bright through narrow slits. These were young airmen, some only seventeen or eighteen years old, all with desperate burn injuries, waiting to go south to a specialist hospital for skin-graft treatment.

"Kitchens" work was demanding, but the social life was more varied than it had been on "house". All day, nurses and patient-orderlies seemed to have some reason for dropping in, and tea was more or less on tap. 6.30 am meant dragging buckets of clinker out of the depths of the vast and venerable coal-burning cooker. This task required one to wear a shower cap and hold one's breath when one crawled to reach the monster's inner maw: it was a somewhat stressful experience.

When a convoy of ambulances was due at the great front door, "house" was banished to the kitchen, well out of the way, and "hospital" swarmed the entrance hall in numbers we never otherwise knew to exist. Once their patients were settled, nurses drifted into the kitchen for the always available tea.

There was usually a degree of depression as they shook heads over the more horrific of the injuries with which they were having to deal. But one afternoon, after the ambulance arrived, there was a remarkable change. The tea-drinking nurses were cheerful and positively twittering: for some reason the phrase "But it's only three weeks!" still rings in my memory. The ambulances had delivered the first cohort of the wounded to have been treated with penicillin. None of us realised this but that afternoon, in the miracle of short-time healing, we were witnessing a herald of a new life-saving age. For good or for ill, the antibiotic era had arrived.

With forty to fifty patients plus nursing, housekeeping and kitchen staff to feed, cooking was on quite a grand scale, and preparation in those days was done by hand. Most of my time went into the cleaning, peeling and trimming of vegetables. Every Thursday was rabbit day and every Friday cod—all arriving duly slaughtered but otherwise strictly *au naturel*. Skinning one's first rabbit is a somewhat traumatising rite of passage, but the successful filleting of a codfish the size of a sofa seat-cushion is deeply satisfying. Happily, we were frequently helped in these "abattoirial" tasks by cheerful teams of ready-for-discharge patients.

These men hacked away at turf and surf with apparent ease,

drank endless mugs of tea and livened up the kitchens with jokes in every UK dialect, from Glasgow to the East End of London. There were always young female kitchen workers around joining in the laughter, but there was not even a hint of sleaze or of what today might be labelled "harassment". Had there been, it could not have passed me by unnoticed; "kitchens" would have made sure of that. There was no way in which hospital discipline could have exercised complete control in these circumstances: it was clearly the currently accepted consensus on time and place, and military hospital kitchens were not an "anything goes" location.

I do not recall any stated rules on smoking, but of the group only "Cook" occasionally relaxed rather elegantly with a Du Maurier (considered a rather refined cigarette), off-duty in the staff sitting room. Presiding over and leading in kitchen activities, "Cook" was a competent, friendly, gracious woman in her forties. She never joined the dining-room meals, but ate casually as she worked. Cook was universally respected and had everything under unruffled control, but she never discouraged the visitors and general social life which accompanied our work. Although apparently from the same sort of background as the others, she had a gamine, almost chic style, and her casually worn white coat overall looked more "hospital" than "kitchen". Altogether, "Cook" emanated more questions than answers. Had she been born a few decades later, she would probably have qualified for a different status in life.

That was true also of some of the scrubbers. Notoriously, the British 1940s (free) Education Act did little for the lumpen proletariat, but these were girls with the kind of grit to make sure that their children moved up and on. Not one of them ever mentioned my schooling, but the kitchen circle included one patient-helper (a peace-time employee from the Ford motor works at Dagenham, notorious for labour strikes) who expressed great bitterness that any girl should have the chance of going to university. All quite friendly and "nothing personal", but only after every boy had college admission should resources be used to provide higher education for girls. His sentiments were somewhat extreme, even for his time, but I hope some post-service provision gave this man the educational opportunities he was clearly able and motivated to use, and which might perhaps also have broadened his outlook.

As a volunteer I was provided with free board and lodging in the hospital, and the return bus fare from my home village. This involved a quite long and complicated journey, with changes at bus terminals of two different towns. There was no honorarium of any kind but no matter, I was provided an educational and maturing experience far more valuable than any cash, and I have always listed this at the head of my curriculum vitae. Interestingly, in my initial application for an academic post, the members of the admissions committee became quite fixated on this item, and the interview morphed into an animated discussion of my subaltern experiences. I do not recall that the more pertinent details of my application received any attention whatsoever, but I was appointed!

3

"Problem of the Aged"?

In the summer of 1953, London saw the splendid coronation of the then twenty-seven-year-old Queen Elizabeth of England. She was attended by train bearers—six young women of noble birth, all around the age of twenty-plus. Sixty years on, during the Queen's Jubilee Year of 2013, she herself was doing pretty well at age eighty-seven. And of the train bearers, five out of the six were not only alive at ages around eighty and above, but were in good enough health to take part in a BBC programme.

These elderly ladies were asked, during the programme, to record their personal memories of that great state occasion of sixty years ago. The listeners were regaled with many amusing anecdotes, for example, about hunger assuaged by Mars bars sneaked into solemn Westminster Abbey under the folds of robes. The programme presenter made good use of these memories, but what of the fact that five out of six of the train-bearers were still quite spry in their eighties? No comment was made on this modern miracle of survival.

We can so easily forget that the present-day incidence of longevity is as much a miracle as the pervasive availability of electronic items which have transformed so many details of our daily life.

My paternal great-grandparents were spoken of with great respect in my family as having raised a family of fourteen children, born between 1839 and 1857, without the loss of even one in babyhood. They were a fairly well-to-do family, able to educate all their eight sons at "public" school, and indeed all fourteen children were still around at age twenty. However, of those fourteen safely reared to adulthood, only two survived to age eighty and above. By age forty, six of the fourteen had already died and all from illness, not one accident or war casualty, and certainly no suicide—my family, on the whole, thought life too entertaining for anything like that to have occurred.

Two unrelated cases with no scientific significance but two out of fourteen, as against six out of seven, does seem like a rather telling contrast between nineteenth- and twenty-first-century survival rates.

My maternal grandparents, in contrast, suffered the then common tragedy of infant mortality. They married in 1866, and by 1870 had three thriving children, all of whom survived well into late adulthood, the eldest to age ninety-three. But between 1870 and 1885 my grandmother gave birth to nine babies, of whom only three survived, six dying under the age of one month. In 1886 her last childbirth produced my feisty mother, who was told she had been fed from birth on "Nestle's milk", presumably what we came to know as sweetened condensed milk.

This fact probably provides a clue to the deaths of the previous six. It was said that my grandmother suffered severe haemorrhage with each birth, in a time when there was no blood transfusion or uterus-shrinking injections to protect women during parturition. This was an era when post-parturition haemorrhage was one cause of maternal death, also, alas, not uncommon.

At least my grandmother always pulled through. But perhaps she was progressively weakened, and while able to breastfeed her first three babies, was, after subsequent births, unable to do so. And this was an age when artificial feeding of the newborn was little developed, and only the toughest babies survived. Sources describe the artificial feeding of babies with crumbled bread, soaked in water to which a little sugar was added (see Flanders 2004). With food of such low nutritional value, it is amazing that any babies survived. True, my grandmother survived her many pregnancies but she died of pneumonia at the relatively young age of forty-seven, which would rarely happen nowadays thanks to antibiotics.

By 1926, the year I was born, knowledge of hygiene had reduced the death rate considerably. But until the general use of antibiotics post World War II, many conditions that we regard as treatable remained life-threatening. Sometime in the 1920s, the fiancé of Beatrice Potter, author of the beloved Peter Rabbit stories, died following a tooth extraction. The site of the extraction became septic, leading to the dreaded and usually fatal septicaemia. A similar fate carried off the much romanticised World War I Cambridge poet, Rupert Brooke. In his case, the undignified cause of death was a septic insect bite on the lip. Nowadays, both men would have been saved by antibiotic medicines.

The life story of the famous Sir Stamford Raffles is "riddled" with early deaths. He was out in Penang and newly married in 1805, aged twenty-four. When he was only thirty-three, his (childless) young wife died. Three years later he remarried, and of this marriage there were five children. Of these five, one died aged two months, two at the age of two years and one at the age of four. The literature usually says that one of the five survived to adulthood but, in fact, she died at the age of nineteen. Moreover, Raffles himself died shortly before his forty-fifth birthday. This pattern of family mortality is inconceivable in the modern developed world.

These examples are all of British people but this pattern of demographic history was worldwide, with less developed countries even more severely affected. In Singapore in 1904, of every 1,000 babies born, 316 died before their first birthday (my figures on mortality are from Manderson 1996). Moreover, officials believed the infant death rate was even higher than this. If a baby died soon after birth, families frequently did not bother to register either the birth or the death.

In Singapore in 1955, on the way back from Welfare Department visits up Yio Chu Kang Road, my car would often be stopped by the traffic light at the T-junction with Upper Serangoon Road. Directly across Upper Serangoon Road the row of shops then included a Chinese undertaker's premises, long gone. This shop was stocked with the enormous whole-tree coffins then customary for Chinese funerals. Looking across from my car as I waited for the green light, I wondered why a coffin shop would also stock a pile of simple plank tool boxes of varied sizes. Only on the third such occasion did it dawn on me that these "tool boxes" were, in fact, children's coffins. Even in 1955, these were in such regular demand that it paid the undertaker to have a ready supply in various sizes. From recent enquiries it seems that the death of a child is now blessedly so rare an occurrence that a coffin would only be made as and when required.

By 1950 the death rate per 1,000 births before a baby's first birthday was down to just under 61. But, and this must be a source of rejoicing, by 2012 that figure had dropped to below two per 1,000.

A great deal of attention is devoted to the "old age problem", and there are indeed genuine concerns about meeting future needs. With low birth rates, only with astronomical rises in productivity can we hope to provide adequate standards of living for all. But we can too easily overlook the fact that underlying this is the wonderful fact of long life, in dramatic contrast to the high rates of early deaths of children and young people which were universals throughout history until the latter half of the twentieth century.

4

An Assortment of Small Graves

In December 1954, one of the passengers on the P&O liner arriving in Singapore was a retired postmistress from a small English country town.

Fifty-plus years previously she had been born and lived until the age of six in Singapore, with her parents and three younger sisters, in the quarters of the old prison. Her father had been a prison warder in the days when these posts were always filled with men recruited from Britain.

This was many years before antibiotic medicine, and when around 1904 a vicious fever attacked children in Singapore, all three of her little sisters had died within two terrible months, and were duly buried in small graves in the Christian cemetery. In those days and until the 1970s, this cemetery occupied the land along Lower Bukit Timah Road, which is now the site of KK Women's and Children's Hospital.

The prison warder and his wife were naturally distraught at this tragic decimation of their little family. The father immediately resigned from his post and rushed his wife and surviving child back to England on the first available ship. They settled back into the

British prisons service. The surviving little girl did well in school and in due course joined the postal service, which in those days was considered a good career for a woman.

The family were devout Christians and therefore had no doubts about the welfare of the souls of their little lost innocents. But the mother, especially, suffered depression at the thought of those three little faraway lonely graves, which she was unable to visit and care for. In the England of that era, regular weekend visits to family graves in the local churchyard was very much part of the culture.

During the mother's last illness, the surviving daughter had comforted the old lady with the promise that when she retired she would make a return visit to Singapore, and visit the cemetery where lay the mortal remains of the three lost little girls. The P&O journey was the fulfilment of that promise

Some time ago, an elderly English friend confided to me a family story which had been told to her by her grandmother, who was the eldest of fourteen children. By the birth of the fourteenth baby, May, the mother was too weak to breastfeed. This was in the 1880s when artificial feeding for babies was at a primitive stage of development: the best solution was to find a wet nurse, a new mother strong enough to provide breast milk for two babies.

The family were wealthy graziers, a business that entailed long-term relationships with a large number of animal-rearing farms. In one of these, the farmer's wife had given birth to a baby girl the same week as May was born. She was a strong and healthy young woman, well able to feed two babies, and was agreeable to act as wet nurse for May, who was duly despatched to be in her care.

This farm was way off in the hills, too far from a made-up road for family members to visit. From time to time one of the grazier's men would ride over on horseback with the "milk fee", and gifts of nourishing supplements for the wet nurse. After some months this man came back with the sad news that the farmer's baby had died, but that May was well and thriving. A condolence gift was sent over and the matter then forgotten.

After weaning time, May returned to the family. Or did she? Was it really she who returned? Or was May the baby lying in the graveyard of that far-off hill village church, and this the farmer's child? What motives could the farmer's family have had for lying? Perhaps fear of the anger of a rich and powerful family, accusations of neglect and lack of care? Or perhaps the "milk fee" was a valuable addition to their modest income? Or had they sought an opportunity for one of their daughters to grow up in circumstances much more favourable than they could provide? Perhaps a combination of all these. The truth could never be known, as this was before the days of DNA and blood grouping, and at that time in history science could not yet provide any firm answers on identity.

The toddler who came down to join the grazier's family was lively and good-natured and fitted in well with the other siblings, but as time passed she grew more and more different from the others in appearance.

As my friend's grandmother was the eldest in the family, she was her mother's confidante and privy to her parents' doubts in the early days of May's return. But from then on these doubts were totally unspoken, and the subject of May's true identity was never once referred to among family members.

Did the grazier father perhaps ride over to view the other children of the farmer to confirm his doubts? No, he did not; this might have proved the equivalent of stepping into a hornets' nest of emotions, too painful to bear. He had eleven fine surviving children out of the fourteen born to him and his wife, a brood big enough to embrace one changeling without too much emotional upheaval. In an era when losing babies was a common if saddening occurrence, attention was best focussed on the large and demanding brood of survivors. The priorities of family life were very different in those faraway days.

Alas, baby deaths were common in all cultures until a better appreciation of the role of hygiene, and then modern medicine, began to provide protection against bacterial diseases. In Chapter 3, there is some data relating to early Singapore; high infant mortality was a universal issue.

In 1952, in the final weeks of a fairly easy pregnancy and in the best of health, I was on my way into the entrance of the old KK Hospital for a routine antenatal check-up. Coming down the entrance steps towards me were three Malay men walking side by side. They had the appearance of brothers, and all wore grim and solemn expressions. The man in the middle had a sarong around his neck and stretched out in front of him, covering his outstretched arms and hands. Under this cover, he seemed to be carrying some sort of tray.

There could be only one possible explanation. The two men on either side of the man in the middle were there to give brotherly support to the bereaved young father as he performed the loving duty of personally bearing his dead baby from the hospital to the burial ground. A sad scenario, but also a wonderful spectacle of what family support can mean when a tragedy occurs. It was the most poignant sight I have ever seen. The babe in me stirred as if in mystical salutation, and that morning my doctor had to deal with a sobbing patient.

In the 1920s, a Chinese couple who were running a small but prosperous grocery and general store in a rural part of Singapore, sadly lost their only child, a much loved little daughter. They arranged for her to be buried in the graveyard used by families of their dialect group, and ensured that her grave was tended to in the way that their customs decreed. It was not easy for them to do this themselves as, according to Chinese custom, those who die young are thereby "unfilial", and an elder paying them attention would be adding to the burden of guilt already carried by the young soul.

Some years later the husband died as well, but a reliable and hard-working young man, who had been an assistant with them in the shop for some years, enabled the widow to carry on the business.

A time came when the widow planned to retire and return to her own people in China. She intended to transfer the business to the faithful assistant. He was delighted at his good fortune and readily agreed to the one condition attached to the transaction: the widow would act as matchmaker and choose a suitable wife for him. In that pre-War era, and for a young man without family of his own to undertake the task, this help with match-making was an added bonus. However, before his marriage to the chosen young woman he would be required to go through a ceremony in which the spirit of the widow's dead little girl would, by what was known then as a ghost marriage, become his first wife. The living bride was to have the status of only a secondary wife. As a young man with a prosperous business he was an eligible match, and all parties readily agreed. The marriage ceremonies for both wives, the dead and the living, were duly carried out, and the widow could then retire to China, confident that she had ensured the welfare of her beloved child.

This story was related to me in the 1950s. My informant noted that, at that date, the grocery store owner and his wife, and their (by then) young adult family still faithfully visited the cemetery where lay the little ghost first wife, and carried out the annual rites proper for their situation. Traditional custom had provided a heart-warming solution in the case of the need for the care of this little grave.

I learned about the sad story of the prison warder's family from my late mother. On her first voyage to Singapore, she and the retired postmistress shared a cabin.

For the story of the changeling babe, I am indebted to a friend who prefers to remain anonymous.

The story of the little ghost wife was narrated to me by the late Mr Roch Goh, who was a mine of information on Teochew customs.

Mainly Singapore: Culture Learning in a New Home

A Life Journey, with this and that Picked Up along the Way

You might say it all began with my St Andrew's Cathedral wedding on 28 June 1950. Shortly after that life-changing event, we learned that for the celebration of our marriage we had stumbled on a most inauspicious date.

On that same day, 28 June, in 1914, the Austrian Archduke Franz Ferdinand and his wife had been assassinated in Sarajevo. This was, in itself, not exactly a happy memory, which was bad enough. But what was much worse was that this assassination precipitated the entirely calamitous World War I. This was famously an appalling conflict which led to the greatest loss of young military lives in all of human history. Even though we were not normally a superstitious couple, we did rather wonder if we had set ourselves up for trouble—not really seriously, but it was a nasty thought! Anyway, as things turned out we lasted fifty-five years, until death did us part.

In early 1950 I had left an England where, though World War II had ended in 1945, food and clothing were still subject to rationing: indeed, rationing continued until 1953. I was fortunate in having a charming coven of elderly aunts who used very few of their clothing coupons. The best of all the wedding presents from these dear ladies had been a collection of coupons which allowed me to assemble a reasonable trousseau of summer clothes in preparation for my voyage to tropical lands.

Given that time in history, my family was surprisingly supportive of my plans to marry beyond most people's comfort zone: cross race marriages were generally frowned upon in those days. The knowledge that both my future parents-in-law had been educated in Britain and that English was known to be their usual household language were reassuring factors. It helped also that my father (whose ideas my mother was usually happy to follow) prided himself on being an independent thinker. "Don't just follow the crowd!" had been a theme in my upbringing. His arranging for the notice of my marriage to be inserted in the "social" column of the local newspaper was a message to all our circle that this marriage was okay by the family.

There was no option for the average civilian to travel by air in those days; England to Singapore was a three-week-plus voyage by ship. And early 1950 was a memorable time to be travelling East, as many interesting Chinese intellectual self-exiles were making that journey back to their homeland. It was but a few months since China had "stood up"—Chairman Mao's momentous words at the point of Communist victory in 1949. In 1950 Mao had not yet made his later big mistakes and many non-Communist Chinese, who had been sickened by the corruption and in-fighting of the Nationalists, were ready to "give this lot a chance". These were the very words later spoken in my presence by a son of the great Singapore non-Communist community leader, Tan Kah Kee, who chose, in 1950, to return to China to serve his ancestral homeland.

In the ship on which I set out, in April 1950, were about a dozen highly educated and scholarly men returning to what, at that point, they saw as a new and hopeful China. There was also one very refined and cultivated Chinese lady, who had been the pianist with the Swiss National Orchestra and had a grand piano stowed away in the hold of the ship. She was planning to offer her services to a conservatory of music in Beijing. This lady's only European language was French, and in the ship's Economy Class I was one of very few British women who had had the advantage of a grammar-school education. My fairly fluent but grammatically unreliable school-level French was well exercised in delightful conversation with this lady during the voyage.

Over the weeks at sea there was much time for socialising, in a group that included several Singaporeans. Towards the end of the voyage, one of the Singaporeans gave wise counsel. Much as we had enjoyed their company, we must not make any effort to write to our friends in China. Singapore was still a British colony, and envelopes with colonial stamps and postmarks might cause trouble for recipients in a Communist state.

In relation to my trousseau, my culture learning began soon after my arrival in Singapore. My pale blue linen suit and silver jewellery had looked rather nice and suitable for my age in England, but my Chinese mother-in-law viewed all this quite differently. Pale blue had a place in the still complicated choreography of Chinese mourning customs while silver jewellery definitely indicated a death in the family and would not do. After the specified, but much argued over, number of months when they must wear black clothes and then black and white, and then grey, mourners could change into blue. A gift of a modest gold bangle and a dress with some pink in the fabric's design soon put things right. But I did regret that nice linen suit!

Another difficulty was earrings. Both my mother-in-law and a kindly, elderly, Chinese-speaking aunt indicated generously that they would like to give me earrings. But there was a problem. Typical of the female English of my generation my ears had never been pierced, while among Singapore girls piercing was a universal, early childhood rite. Though pressured by my mother-in-law, my physician father-in-law declined to touch my ears. He claimed that doctors always pierced ears unevenly and that a jeweller would do a much better job: as a doctor, he would step in to treat my ears should there be any difficulty in healing.

Once I started teaching at the Methodist Girls' School (MGS), the ear-piercing problem was soon solved. A Teochew colleague was delighted to take me to a jeweller of her own dialect group, and trusted by her family, on Arab Street. The jeweller sat me on a stool on the pavement outside his shop. He took a piece of ginger root and a bottle of TCP, the equivalent of Dettol in those days. He cut the ginger root with a clean knife and held the freshly cut edge firmly against the back of my ear, dipped his needle in the TCP and in no time the job was done, and little gold sleepers inserted.

This ear-piercing procedure had unintentionally provided an occasion of street theatre, and quite a crowd had gathered. The performance was intrinsically interesting, and this was an end of Arab Street to which no tourist would have ventured, so my very person added to the general theatricality. The outcome was excellent—my ears healed promptly and I was gifted a small shower of delightful earrings, which I treasure to this day.

That teaching post at MGS was the best thing that could have happened to me, though, foolishly at first, I resisted the appointment. My in-laws' neighbours were a family of some standing in the local Methodist Church, well aware that at that time MGS had a serious shortage of staff. One teacher had been awarded an overseas scholarship, another had become chronically unwell and a third had been poached by the colonial Education Department to head one of the many new schools being opened at that time.

Our neighbour approached my mother-in-law, pointing out that I was, at the time, just at home, whereas I could be making myself useful by taking up one of the vacant teaching posts. I had found relief teaching in unruly London primary schools so stressful—it served as a means of supplementing my income while in graduate school—that I was reluctant to face a classroom once more. But my refusal to apply was clearly going to embarrass my in-laws, so I went ahead and, in late 1950, took the plunge. This proved to be the most pleasurable possible means of my own education, in what it meant to be a middle-class Singaporean.

Filling in for a more specialist colleague who needed a year away to finish a university course, I was tasked to take the English language and literature lessons in what we would now call the class preparing to take O-levels, then known as the Senior Cambridge. Unlike my boisterous London primary-school pupils, this class was a delight to teach. The students were markedly overage, as they had lost four years of schooling because of the War. They were mostly aged eighteen or nineteen and at least one was already twenty-one, and could be described almost as ravenous learners: my task was more that of coach than teacher. Fortunately, they all passed that vital public-examination hurdle, and many of them went on to become teachers themselves: one indeed, later on, became a much respected principal of MGS.

After the English specialist teacher returned, for the next three happy years I taught in Standard 7, the equivalent of the present Secondary 3. These classes were more demanding, but the students were also both responsive and lively. Some of these pupils, in their later, adult life, became my valued personal friends.

Perhaps even more memorable than the teaching experience were the friendships and culture-learning opportunities afforded by the staffroom social life. A much liked American missionary soon left for service in Malacca, leaving the MGS upper-school staffroom populated entirely by teachers who were local-born Chinese. They were friendly and welcoming, and I learned a great deal from them during coffee-time and free-period conversations.

An early memory of a cultural surprise for me was an attitude to jewellery that was quite contrary to that which I had learned in my natal home. In middle-class England, young women never spent money on gold or diamonds. At a twenty-first birthday, parents might gift their daughter a gold watch or perhaps a finger-ring with opals or pearls. Only when engaged to be married would the fiancé be expected to provide a ring with diamonds or other precious stones, and these might feature in wedding presents but not necessarily so. Personal decoration was mainly a matter of costume jewellery, of which most young women would probably have a fair collection from presents at birthdays or Christmas, or from personal shopping.

To my amazement, my women friends in Singapore regarded costume jewellery as a wild extravagance, as it had no value. A wise young woman was expected to invest in jewellery of real value as a form of asset accumulation. From the early days of my staffroom membership, I recall vividly a criticism hurled by one of my colleagues at an absent teacher acquaintance: "She's been working ten years and she hasn't a single diamond!" It took me some time to digest the meaning of this. Accompanying a colleague on an expedition to buy a piece of gold jewellery assisted in my cultural learning. The jeweller's bill was in two parts, one the cost of the amount of gold and other the cost of the workmanship—the latter was seen as the extravagance. The simpler the workmanship, the more the purchase was a matter of wise asset-building. Several times, I heard tales of how jewellery as an asset had helped the owners during the War, when earning income had been a problem.

Much has been written regarding the switch in status which was taking place in the Malayan and Singapore Chinese communities around that time. Roughly speaking, up to World War II, the Straits-born had regarded their culture as superior to that of the immigrant Chinese. China in the early 20th century was almost a failed state, with law and order broken down, and warlords in endless fights for power. But around the time of the Pacific War, with the Nationalist Government of China being treated as one of the "Allied Great Powers", the global status of China rose. Maurice Freedman, my senior classmate at the London School of Economics, describes this as leading to the Straits Chinese "re-Sinifying", and I witnessed this in action amongst my teacher friends.

Not one of these friends would have dreamed of wearing sarong-kebaya, the normal everyday dress of the mothers of several of my colleagues, and which these older women would have worn when they were young. On a social occasion one of these sarong-clad mothers said in my presence, in the Peranakan patois which was translated for my benefit, "When I was a girl we looked down on those China women in pyjama suits, and called them kitchen skivvies. Now they look down on us, and call us natives." I was told that she used a most offensive Hokkien word for "native". My colleague, who was this lady's daughter, invariably wore the most impeccable cheongsam, as did most of the teachers. When I related this incident to Freedman (who was at the time researching in Singapore), he was fascinated. I well recall his response, "You have witnessed the history of culture change on the hoof!" he laughed.

The advantages of the cheongsam over the sarong-kebaya were often spoken of, especially since the latter, with brooch requirements for the kebaya, was much more expensive. In preparation for Chinese New Year, it was customary for many of my colleagues to have fifteen cheongsam tailored, one for each day of that two-week festival. I recall large tailors' shop boxes containing these being opened at the staffroom coffee table to general plaudits and expressions of admiration.

On reflection, it is surprising how much staffroom conversation was devoted to discussing and arguing over the correct etiquette of mourning wear. In descending order of intensity, one started with sackcloth at the funeral, and moved to black for everyday wear from then on. When was black-and-white acceptable? How long after could one change into grey? And then blue? Or was it green before or after blue? There was much argument over such issues. And for how long should one mourn?

I described this centring of so much dispute on the subject of mourning to Freedman. He saw this arguing and uncertainty as a sign that mourning customs were moving on from a mainstream cultural position, that this aspect of cultural tradition was, in the foreseeable future, "on the way out". And in the twenty-first century, this would indeed seem to be so. For many Singapore families, however filial, the outward trappings of formal mourning last only through the formalities of the funeral.

From those staffroom conversations about correct behaviour in relation to mourning I learned, to my surprise, that "one year" was not in all situations a period comprising twelve months. If an elder died in, say, the tenth month of the Chinese calendar, then by the coming Chinese New Year's Day one had completed one year of mourning. And soon after the following CNY, one could be regarded as completing three years of mourning. But there lay a great source of argument: How long after that following CNY were the three years completed? The consensus settled more or less upon the Dragon Boat Festival of the fifth month of the Chinese year; as I recall, "You must not mourn past a second fifth month."

In matters of mourning, difference in dialect-group customs could cause tensions to the point of flare-up. When a Hokkien married woman whose own parents were still alive was required to perform mourning rites for her parents-in-law, in the arm-band of her sackcloth garments would be sewn a very small square of red cloth. In some mystical way, this was regarded as necessary in order to protect her natal family from the pollution of death. But this custom is completely unknown in Teochew culture. A recently bereaved Teochew colleague became almost incandescent as she described her family's feelings when a Hokkien sister-in-law arrived complete with a little red patch on her sackcloth sleeve. Red at a funeral was completely unthinkable, an anathema to any right-thinking Teochew family. As several sons were available to perform the required rites, the husband of the offensive young Hokkien lady wisely bundled his wife safely towards the back, where her objectionable red patch was out of sight.

After four happy years of rich learning at MGS, at the end of 1954 I was offered a post in the (colonial) Social Welfare Department

(SWD), then located on Havelock Road, in the building which, in 2016, houses the Family Justice Courts.

My years at MGS had trained me for a reasonably competent membership of the Singapore English-educated middle class, a population group for whom Singapore was a fairly comfortable place to be in in the 1950s. SWD exposed me to learning about those for whom Singapore life was rarely comfortable and was mostly a struggle on many different fronts.

In 1945, with the end of the World War, the colonial government was ready for change. Prior to the War, the poor in my home country, Britain, had received very little welfare, and deprivation was far from being a uniquely colonial phenomenon. The post-War Labour Party government in Britain moved towards the welfare state to right wrongs on the home front. Linked with this policy direction was a greater sense of duty to provide care in colonial territories. In June 1946 the Department of Social Welfare in Singapore was established, which took over what had been the duties of the Chinese Protectorate, but with much wider responsibilities to implement social service legislation and policies.

Historically, the building in Havelock Road had housed the Chinese Protectorate and even in 1955 (when it housed both the Labour and Social Welfare Departments), that former occupancy somehow lingered on in the local collective memory. For example, if after a visit in the town area the best means of returning to the office was by trishaw, one needed to say "Pik-ki-lin" to instruct the trishaw rider as to the destination. This was a phonetic distortion of the surname of the first Chinese Protector, William Pickering, who served in Singapore from 1870–97. He was memorable as the first-ever British colonial officer to speak any Chinese—and he spoke a whole range of dialects. His capacity to communicate with them directly so impressed the immigrant community that he acquired a unique and unforgettable status. Apart from Raffles, he was the only colonial officer whose memory became part of the local culture (see

Jackson 1965: a biography of William Pickering, the first officer designated Protector of Chinese, it is highly recommended).

The two years, 1955–6, when I worked in the SWD, brought with them both friendship and learning. Much of that learning was followed up in the research projects of students I worked with on joining the then University of Malaya in 1957. This learning features in later chapters and needs no place here.

The University of Malaya, located in Singapore, was, until 1960, indeed the university serving the whole Malayan peninsula, along with the states of Sabah and Sarawak. The University of Singapore, founded in 1960, continued to provide training for professional social work for this wider region until 1974, when Universiti Sains Malaysia set up a department including this discipline. Therefore, until 1974, the social-work student body in Singapore included Malaysians.

As the diploma course admitted only mature students with working experience, this student body included a range of interesting people. Until 1974, we had regular access to settings for long-vacation field practice placements in Malaya. The social-work training requirement that staff visit students during their placements therefore included not only visits to social-service agencies in Singapore but also long journeys for some staff, taking up one to two weeks every long vacation.

In May 1957, when I undertook the long-vacation field practice supervision, two visits to Malaya were especially memorable. One student had been placed in the State Social Welfare Office in Kota Bharu, Kelantan. By a pleasant coincidence, the State Social Welfare Officer, Raja Abdul Jalil, who was originally from Perak, had been my fellow student at the London School of Economics, so this visit was socially also a happy occasion.

Following the student-focussed business of the visit, my host kindly took me to the homes of the handloom weavers for whose work, among other handicrafts, Kelantan is uniquely famous. In August 1957 Malaya was about to gain independence and would, from then on, cease to be a British colony. At the time of my visit I was privileged to witness the loom of Hajah Che Bidor, the senior of all the weavers; she was preparing the magnificent black-and-gold-thread silk to be worn at the independence ceremonies by the Malayan king, the Yang Di-Pertuan Agung. This was a memorable sight.

We also visited the "social enterprise" retail shop in Kota Bharu, where locally made handicrafts were on sale. While we were speaking with the English woman who was the manager of the shop, an old countryman came in with a cloth bundle balanced on his turban-like head covering. He squatted on the floor and opened his bundle, displaying ten Malay-style daggers (*keris*), the buffalo-horn handles of which he had carved with attractive designs. The manager informed us that this was an activity associated with the season when there was no work required in the rice fields. The daggers were sharp and rather menacing in appearance. Speaking in fluent Malay, the manager asked the elderly man how he had dared walk past the nearby police station with a load of such weapons, which at the time men were forbidden to carry. His reply was ironic and caused laughter all round, including the old man's, "Oh madam, I wouldn't dare walk past the police carrying one *keris*, but ten are alright."

The second student's placement was in a very different setting. He was working with an officer of the Department of Aborigines' Affairs in the state of Pahang. To visit him I had to spend a night at the rest house in Kuala Lipis, a town which is way up the great Pahang River. Early the next morning, the student and several members of the Aborigines' Department staff collected me, and we boarded a small boat with an outboard engine. Our journey was soon off the main river and into a small tributary, up which we travelled for more than two hours, stopping when we came to a clearing.

This clearing was the site of the settlement we were visiting. It comprised a number of lean-to shelters which were the homes of a hunter-gatherer group who called themselves Semoq Beri. Their economy, I was told, was among the least developed of all the aborigine groups known to the Aborigines' Department. The men were mostly out at the time of our visit, while the women and children lounged around rather listlessly. For some reason which the staff could not explain, the children of one family were markedly more plump and lively than the others. Many years later I read that it has been found that in hunter-gatherer groups, if a household includes a post-menopausal woman, the children are always healthier and have better physical development. I wish I had learned this before that visit, as it would have guided my questions on household composition. Clearly a case of "Hurrah for grandma!"

After 1974 we retained friendly links with many of our Malayan graduates, but the work became more Singapore-centred.

Perhaps I gained my own learning experience most intensely from my work as an advisor to the Juvenile Court. Dating from colonial times, when the magistrate was likely to be from Britain, Juvenile Court legislation has required that the magistrate should be aided by two advisors. The role of the advisor has been to bring a wider range of local knowledge to decisions on appropriate treatment of the young offender or a youngster deemed "beyond parental control" or "in need of care and protection", the three categories of problems in which the court has jurisdiction.

In tribute to the system, I should mention that great efforts are made to deal with these problems without resort to the court. The police have developed a system of dealing with minor offences by assessing, from the reaction of parents and the report from the school, if this is likely to be a one-off incident of offensive behaviour. Where deemed appropriate, a solemn warning is administered and the case closed. Records have shown that in more than two-thirds of the warned cases, these youngsters keep clear of further trouble.

When a parent complains to the court that a child is beyond parental control, the case is referred to the Singapore Children's

Society, gazetted to undertake family-case work, which enables many such families to acquire competence in problem-solving. In cases where a child is not receiving adequate care, the staff of the ministry makes every effort to arrange appropriate provision informally. Therefore only the most severely problem cases are ever seen by the court.

From two to four months of each year from 1971 to 2009, as an advisor I was required to read through the case papers prepared by ministry staff who had investigated the situations of the youngsters and made tentative proposals about what seemed to them to be the wisest treatment. By far the greatest number of cases were those involving boys who had committed criminal offences, most often offences against property. Roughly generalising, in the 1970s the problem was theft of bicycles; by the year 2000 it was hand phones. Therefore my most frequent contact was with probation officers (POs), from whose interesting and often thoughtful reports I was kept in touch, over the years, with the situation of families facing difficulties in managing their young.

I came to admire greatly the POs' capacity to prepare a number of case reports for presentation in court in a relatively short period of time. This involved contact with the school, sometimes also with an employer, with parents and even with any member of the extended family who had the potential to help. For example, where the father stated that an uncle was willing to house the boy during the school week, the PO then had to contact the uncle—and also the aunt! This range of necessary contacts meant that the POs always had to be prepared to make visits during "unsociable hours". The commitment to duty required in a career in the probation service is not always appreciated. But I also have a very personal reason for remembering the POs' kindness.

On my last day on duty in the Juvenile Court, near the end of 2009, I received a message asking if I could spare a moment to drop in at the senior PO's office after the session. On my way to the lift, I remember hoping she was not going to land me with some burdensome writing chore. I need not have worried. As I got out of the lift I caught sight, through her open door, of a PO raising a glass. Whoops, I had been invited to a farewell party! They had taken the trouble to organise a splendid gathering on this occasion and to put together a great collection of photographs and kind messages for me as a memento of all the years we had worked together. This was indeed a farewell in a cloud of fairy dust.

Despite starting off as something of an adopted daughter in this and in many other ways, I have received, over the years, much kindness and acceptance as a "card-carrying member of the Singapore club".

6

Glimpses of World War II: One Man Moves On from a Massacre

Within weeks of my joining the Methodist Girls' School (MGS) in late 1950, there was much rejoicing in the staffroom over an impending wedding. A gentle and well-liked colleague, aged thirty-two, was to marry a widower in his early forties and in a good position. In those days, thirty-two was considered an unusually late age for a young woman to marry, unlike the general standard of later age at the first marriage in the present century. I remember the colleague smiling in mild embarrassment and referring to herself as "an old bride".

As things turned out, this proved to be a very successful union: several fine children were born, the parents both lived to old age and the children, as well-established and married adults, all chose to buy property in the same parental neighbourhood, indicating warm relationships. But at the birth of the first child there had been some minor problems.

As colleagues of the mother, we heard how the new father was so protective and anxious about the safety of his little son, that he insisted that everything to do with baby care must be cleaned in alcohol. The family's GP had mentored this situation and counselled the father that this extreme cleanliness would, in fact, endanger the child, as it would prevent the development of a healthy immune system.

In staffroom natter, it was regarded as not surprising that this good man was an overprotective father. It was in the light of this incident that my colleagues confided in me the story of the ghastly tragedy that had left the father a widower in the first place. His first wife and four children had been slaughtered in one of the inexplicable massacres of civilians which happened mainly in Johor, in the course of the Japanese Army's early weeks of the conquest of Malaya.

The father had grown up in an extended family living beside their fruit orchard and within easy commuting distance from Johor Bahru, where he and his brother had careers in the colonial civil service. At the news of the advance of the Japanese army, the widowed grandmother happened to be staying elsewhere in Johor, visiting her kin. The father and his married brother had gone to ensure that their mother was safe, leaving their younger bachelor brother and the women and children at the orchard home, which had seemed to be well away from any main road.

This estimate was a tragic mistake: the two men returned to the orchard to a scene of slaughter. The bloodied corpses of the three adults and eight children were scattered around the family home. Somehow or other these bereaved men faced life again, and after eight years of mourning, my colleague's husband felt able to resume family life.

As this new family's children were around the same age as my children and went to the same school, we were in touch during their childhood. Many years later, I attended the wake of their widowed mother, my erstwhile dear colleague, and renewed my acquaintanceships. When the oldest son was well over fifty, he and I happened to attend the same all-day seminar and had the pleasure of chatting over coffee. In this setting I ventured to ask him a very personal question, at which he was kind enough to not take offence.

My question to him was regarding how his father's appalling tragedy in his young adult life had affected the children of his second marriage. To my amazement the answer was, "Not at all." Only after their father's death, by which time they were all adults, had their mother related to them the tragic story. This strong and caring man had borne his burden of memory alone, to ensure that the past cast no shadow over the new family's childhood years.

No doubt the father's Chinese culture provided him with models of this pattern of dealing with grief. Indeed, where children themselves have suffered bereavement, this cultural model can cause problems by preventing the mourning response, which can be an important part of the recovery process. I recall that probation officers sometimes faced this problem in their cases, where they had to help a bereaved youngster to allow himself to weep over his loss of a parent. But in the case of a bereaved adult protecting his children, as in this family, one can only feel respect for his inner strength.

When preparing to write about this family, I felt the need for some reading references on the several never explained Japanese massacres of civilians in Malaya, mainly in Johor, during the early weeks of the conquest. I learned, from consultation with a senior historian of that period, that so far there has been no systematic research or documentation of these tragic events.

In *Playing for Malaya: A Eurasian Family in the Pacific War* (2012), Rebecca Kenneison documents her systematic research on one incident which involved some of her relatives. This was the slaughter of about sixty Selangor Eurasians making their way south as refugees, and gathered for shelter at a rubber estate near Ulu Tiram in Johor. The author even researched the documents of a Catholic priest in a museum in Britain. This priest was the only literate witness but again, there was no credible explanation for this appalling rampage. Active NUS Senior Alumnus Donald Wyatt, who was born in Kuantan, Pahang, recalls that as a small boy, his family were also refugees making their way south. They also rested at Ulu Tiram but, fortunately for them, the father felt it would be wiser to move on to Singapore.

In the early months of the Japanese occupation of Singapore, the army perpetrated the notorious "Sook Ching" massacre of tens of thousands of middle-class men, including two brothers of my mother-in-law. This was said to be the elimination of the possible leaders of an uprising in their rear, when the main Japanese Army regiments moved on to the Sumatran oil fields, a priority objective of the push into Southeast Asia. A somewhat comparable massacre took place along the seafront in Johor Bahru—as documented in Lim Pui Huen's chapter titled "War and Ambivalence: Monuments and Memorials in Johor" in *War and Memory in Malaysia and Singapore* (2000)—causing horrendous long-term pollution of a widespread fishing area.

In the course of the three-and-a-half years of Japanese Occupation, many Singaporeans could recall decency and even kindness on the part of individual Japanese. My mother-in-law recalled that a Japanese housewife in Balmoral Road would, from time to time, send her Malay kitchen helper to call at the backdoor of households on the same road. The message was that there would be a pile of bags of sugar (or other dry items) at the backdoor of the Japanese family's home that evening, to which the neighbours were welcome to help themselves. This was much appreciated help in a time of shortage. Distinguished botanist E.J.H. Corner has written of the scholarly Marquis Tokugawa, who insisted that the valuable biological research carried on in Singapore's Botanic Gardens must not be interrupted by the War (see Corner 1981). The widespread life-saving and welfare activities of the English-educated Momaru Shinozaki make for heartwarming reading (Shinozaki 1973). But the initial months of the Occupation left such a trail of innocent blood that it took some time for Singaporeans and Malayans to come to terms with this and move on (see Kenneison 2012).

Students and staff of the Department of Social Work, NUS, after convocation, early 1960s (Photo credit: Department of Social Work, NUS).

Party on the occasion of the visit of Professor Gore, external examiner from India, to the Department of Social Work, NUS, late 1950s (Photo credit: Department of Social Work, NUS).

With Mrs and Mr S.R. Nathan, 1980s (Photo credit: Department of Social Work, NUS).

Street scene after the war, 1940s and 1950s (Photo credit: Student community project).

Student community group project. Interviewing a stallholder, 1970s (Photo credit: Author's personal collection).

TOP AND BELOW: Henry Park area, 1955 (Photo credit: Author's personal collection).

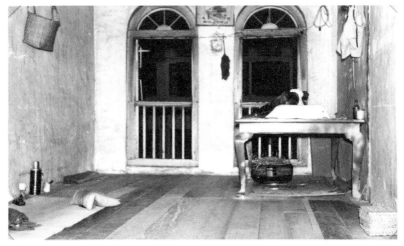

A resident is sleeping on a fixed table-like structure (Photo credit: Francis Tan, "Teochew Kongsi Houses in Singapore", academic exercise (Singapore: Department of Social Work and Social Administration, University of Singapore, 1963).

A close view of a sleeping space and the resident's personal belongings (Photo credit: Francis Tan, "Teochew Kongsi Houses in Singapore", academic exercise (Singapore: Department of Social Work and Social Administration, University of Singapore, 1963).

Slum housing in Singapore (including a rat!) (Photo credit: Alice Yeo, student project, late 1960s)

7

Children and Childhood in the Singapore Chinese Family: An Experience of Culture Learning

In the mid–1950s, two little Singapore Chinese sisters were bathed, suppered and into their pyjamas by the time their father returned home late from the family business. At the sound of his car in the driveway, they trotted out to meet him. And over a long period during their childhood, a much enjoyed and nostalgically recalled, nightly choral ritual (in Hokkien dialect) ensued. Their father would slump down in a lounge chair, with an arm around each snuggling daughter.

"Why is Papa late?" he would ask, opening the chorale.
"Papa is late because he works very hard."
"Why does Papa work very hard?"
"Papa works very hard to earn money."
"Why does Papa need to earn money?"
"So that we can have a good life."
"Why does Papa want you to have a good life?"
"Because Papa loves us." (*An exchange of hugs*)

"And when you grow up?"

"We will cook Papa a nice, tasty dish of pork."

(*General dissolving into hugs and giggles, and then off to bed.*)

In the 1960s, one of these two (then teenage) sisters recalled this family ritual with much amusement. By the norms of his times "Papa" was a modern father, demonstratively affectionate towards his children when they were young, and ensuring that his daughters had the same educational opportunities as their brothers when the time came. But there was still the theme that parental love involves sacrifice; sacrifice which would be repaid by the children later.

In this particular family the lesson was instilled in a teasing, affectionate manner, but frequently it was articulated in much more blunt terms. Undeniably, children learned early, and in no uncertain terms, that they were indebted to their parents, who suffered hardship and made sacrifices in order to bring them up. Because of this the children incurred the lifelong responsibility of repaying this debt.

In countries where there are no government-regulated and/or other organised systems of preparing for old age, children have always been, and still are, virtually the only social insurance system around. But perhaps because of the "afterlife component", the non-Christian Chinese family blueprint included an unusually articulate emphasis on filial piety, to ensure that the lesson was learned well and learned young. The parents' wellbeing depended on the care afforded them by children not only during their old age in this world, but also in their afterlife. In the afterlife one needed the rituals performed by filial male descendants: if these were lacking, the destiny of becoming a homeless ghost in the Chinese afterlife was too horrible to contemplate.

An early observation, soon after my arrival in Singapore in 1950, also threw some light on this theme of child training. This related to the manner in which mothers and children crossed streets together. I recalled, in my own English childhood, negotiating the hazards of crossing the road, mutually clasping hands with my mother. I had hitherto neither witnessed nor dreamed of any other possible method. But the Singapore mother, in contrast, grasped her child's wrist in a manner which left the little hand dangling and passive. "Yes," said my Singapore friends when I commented on this, "that way is much safer." Was this degree of safety truly needed, I pondered. I did not recall that the hand clasp to which I had been accustomed had resulted in a high rate of child mortality on the roads. Clearly, the difference related to something more than the preservation of the child's life.

I recollected this difference in road-crossing technique when I came to have small children of my own, in the 1950s, and was warned, not once but on numerous occasions, not to "chit-chat" with my pre-schoolers or they would (and I quote) "take advantage" and "not respect you". For friends and acquaintances who gave me such advice, parenting was perhaps not training in reciprocity but a controlling, "top-down" activity, in which the establishment of the attitude of healthy respect on the part of the children towards their elders was a priority element in the parenting "mission statement". Those passive, dangling little hands fit into this picture.

Further insights on the absence of parent–child "chit-chat" came from the 1951 survey referred to in Chapter 8, where one of the sample families happened to live in a Soh-lineage village. Each family interviewed in that survey had a child who attended one of the Children's Social Centres (CSC). These were organised by the Social Welfare Department for children unable to find a place in a mainstream school—the insufficiency of school places being a worrying problem in the decade following the end of World War II.

The CSCs, each run by one paid staff and a team of volunteers, provided a nourishing meal, rather amateur attention to literacy and numeracy, and marked attention to education on health and nutrition. The objective of the survey was to enquire if this health and nutrition education was impacting the practices of the children's families. The findings of the survey proved dismally disappointing and showed no impact whatsoever. The parents were appreciative of the meal provided, and glad of the attention to literacy and numeracy. Apart from these things, they had no knowledge of, nor any interest whatsoever in, their children's activities at the Centre. Parent–child informal chatting was not a feature of the family life of those times.

Another early culture-learning experience with regard to family came through my being required, in late 1950, to conduct an oral English examination for girls aged thirteen or fourteen at Methodist Girls' School. In the interest of standardisation, I was provided with a list of questions with which to initiate this mutual ordeal. "How many brothers and sisters do you have?" If the answer was, for example, "six", I, the newly arrived, western-reared examiner not unnaturally envisaged a brood of seven children. But this was cross-cultural ignorance. My young examinee did not see herself as an individual with a number of siblings but as a member of a group of six. The focus was on the group, not on herself, a subtle but very real distinction which provided me with an introduction to the structured and corporate character of the Chinese family.

This learning was reinforced as I came to work for four years in the same school, and enjoyed close friendships with the staffroom crowd. During coffee-break conversation my (mainly Straits-born Chinese) colleagues made frequent reference to their brothers and sisters. Yet never once, over the entire four years, did I learn the names of even one of their siblings. It was always "my second brother" or "my third sister". These relationships were often warm and close, but siblings were clearly seen as members of a structure rather than as named individuals.

Some scholars have likened the historic Chinese family blueprint or model to a corporation, with the parent "CEOs" training the sons for future managerial roles, and, in the case of girls, the parents preparing them for subordinate roles in another corporate group, and a group not of the girls' own choosing. Family "corporate" advantage, not individual feelings, would be the basis on which the match would be made.

This model fits a top-down parent–child relationship, cautious in demonstrative affection or in the familiarity of "chit-chat", which could interfere, on the part of the young, with the development of healthy respect for their elders (the "family managers"). Those youngsters were, in a sense, apprentices in training.

This model also helps explain the generally observed low level of emotional involvement with daughters in historic China. In her early teens, tradition decreed that the daughter must be sent as a bride to another "family corporation", usually a great distance away. Henceforth, her natal family would be unable to help their daughter in any way, even if she received harsh treatment in her new home. In these circumstances, deep emotional commitment to a beloved child one was helpless to defend would have been a recipe for endless parental misery, indeed for depressive mental ill-health. In the words of one scholar, the Chinese family gave up access to their daughters' wellbeing in exchange for full control of daughters-in-law and wives.

Faraway marriages were not usual in the South Seas, but it took some generations for a change in attitudes to daughters. In the same girls' school to which I have referred, I recall the feisty principal (the great Ellice Handy of cookery-book fame; see Bibliography), having furious arguments at the threshold of her office, in Malay, with Peranakan mothers. Mrs Handy was always trying to dissuade these mothers from taking their daughters out of school before the completion of their secondary education. The usual argument, on the part of the mothers, and which was repeated on numerous occasions, was that by her early twenties the girl would marry, and (I quote) "those other people" would reap the benefits from the money spent on her schooling by her own parents. Family priorities, not the individual development of one family member, must come first.

Even then, in Singapore and among the Straits Chinese,

daughters were still, to some extent, considered as "goods on which you lose". They were yours only temporarily, until they fulfilled their destiny as members of their husbands' families.

And only as a mother in her husband's family was a woman assured of filial care in this world and the next. Once married, she and her children had no part in the ancestor worship of her natal family. Only as a mother of sons was her own wellbeing in old age and in the Chinese afterlife assured: only her sons and her sons' children could look after her when she became old, and tend to the needs of her soul after her death.

This distinction was brought home to me when I worked in the Social Welfare Department in 1955–6. I was asked to interview an elderly Peranakan Chinese lady who had appealed to her married son's multinational employer to transfer him back from Kuala Lumpur to Singapore, on the grounds that she missed her grandchildren. In the course of our (Malay-language) conversation it arose that in Singapore she was close to her five married daughters, all of whom had children who visited her often. "But Bebe," I explained, using the form of address correct for this lady's age, "with all those grandchildren around, it will be difficult for your son's employer to accept that you are lonely." Her reply came at me like a cannonball: "Those are not mine! Those are other people's grandchildren!" The look of utter bewilderment on the lady's face, that I should have failed to see this from the outset, resulted in a most profound cross-cultural learning experience for me.

Confucian restraint in physical demonstrations of love and affection in family life has often been interpreted by casual western observers as a sign of coldness in family relationships. Their own growing-up experience has made it difficult for westerners to envisage any way of expressing love other than in its articulation, as well as the hugging model of body contact with which they are familiar. Adherence to this model in seeking to understand Chinese family life can mean that one may miss the indicators of caring and warmth well understood within Chinese culture.

My dear (and, sadly, long gone) friend Dr Chin Ai Li, described coming home from morning school in Shanghai in the 1920s and announcing to her father that she was top of her class. "Humph," he said, and went on reading his newspaper. But at the lunch table he announced casually that the family would be eating at a restaurant that evening. Nothing further was said but around the table, the mother and children exchanged sly smiling glances which the father ignored. Even in her old age, Ai Li recalled a physical sensation of warmth and joy and a sense of being valued, praised and cared for: no less real for the roundabout way in which she had received, from her father, the message of parental love and approval.

Before Ai Li recalled this incident in her own life, I had described to her my own visit, in 1950, to the wards of St Andrew's Mission Children's Hospital, which was then situated in one of the poorest slum districts in Singapore's Chinatown. The visiting hour arrived and in trooped the mothers (many, as I recall, looking worn and shabbily attired), each carrying a small tiffin carrier of cooked food.

To the amazement of my culturally ignorant eyes, not one mother kissed or hugged her child. She felt the child's forehead, perhaps squeezed the upper arm but pretty promptly sat down on the bedside stool and began coaxingly to feed her sick child with chicken, either as porridge or prepared in some other way.

This was long before the introduction of factory-style poultry rearing and chicken was still very much a luxury food, appearing on poor tables only at Chinese New Year, if then. So the message conveyed to the child was very clear: "My mother has spared cash to buy and cook a chicken for me. Wow, I am really important to her, and she really cares for me!"

Food as the language of love emerges in families in Singapore as a recurring theme in those times, and keeps popping up and is still with us. Around 2009, a probation officer was striving to improve relations between a sulky teenager and a fond but inarticulate father who had come to the office to discuss this problem. Discovering that father and son watched football on television together (in cold silence!), the PO suggested that the father might buy some snacks for his son. The PO related to me how the usually sullen boy came beaming to his next reporting session. "My dad bought me a packet of crisps!" Love in action!

Even when one has read and learned about Confucian group orientation in family life, individual examples come as something of a surprise when first encountered on the hoof. In the late 1960s, Chinese and English education were still provided in totally separate school systems. A then fresh graduate from Nanyang Chinese University (now Dr) Lee Chong Kau came to attend social-work training at the (then) University of Singapore. He chose as his research topic an open-ended study of factors which led families (quite a large sample involving four schools) to choose either Chinese or English education for their children. Both he and myself as his supervisor anticipated that parental choices would be on an "either/or" basis. We thought we would find out the reasons why the children of a particular family were all enrolled in one or the other system, and why the parents who would be interviewed regarded one system as superior to the other.

In many families we found a much more complex situation, in which one stream was felt to be far superior but where the needs of the family, as a group, required that one child should be sent to the other stream. "Chinese education is much the best, but we need someone in the family to cope with government letters." Or, "Nowadays English education leads to better prospects, but we need one family member who can keep up the correspondence with the relatives in China."

The analysis did not allow for identifying any gender or birth-order bias in the choice of the sacrificial lamb selected for the "less good" school experience. Nor did we encounter any embarrassment that the family was deliberately depriving one child of what they themselves regarded as the best education. The parental responsibility was to do what was best for the family as a whole. The family, not the individual member, must always come first.

As the Singapore family changes under the impact of economic and other influences, it seems that cultural differences between East and West become somewhat reduced. In each society the family continues to have a certain distinct cultural "flavour", but differences are no longer so extreme.

The little girls in my initial anecdote are now in their late fifties and they and their brothers have, indeed, metaphorically, cooked the "nice dish of tasty pork" for their parents, which they promised "Papa" so long ago. Economic developments have taken some family members overseas but those still around, while not living under the same roof, keep in constant touch, and provide the care and arrangement-making assistance now needed for their parents. In fact, what they are providing is very much the caring, case-management role which is still a recognised feature of adult child–elderly parent relationships in the developed West.

Confucian and western families do start from different basic premises, as the exigencies of their historical, political, economic and social contexts have prescribed. Upbringing in each system has ensured survival, and has proved to come with in-built mechanisms for coping with change, and even with disaster and crisis management.

But rapid change has rarely been experienced as an ongoing and accepted way of life as it is today. Services to help build strength and resilience in children have never been more needed. Helping children cope in an age of change means helping children in their family setting, for we can only truly meet needs if we work systemically (see Wee 2016).

Side by side with service, the study of how families of all cultures cope with this world situation must be another priority, in the interests of not only children, but of us all.

8

The Early Days of the Singapore Family

One of our more profound beliefs in contemporary Singapore is that "the family is the basic building block of society". But that certainly was not the case in Singapore's early days. Right through until the 1920s our population growth stemmed from massive in-migration of single people, mainly of men from India and China, and for the most part they were young, poor and alone.

The dreams of these migrants were of earning enough savings to return to their village in their homeland, to secure a wife and the respected village status of family man. The young men who came to Singapore from what are now West Malaysia and Indonesia also tended to be "long-term commuters", who looked forward to family life elsewhere. Only in the small, local-born Malay and Eurasian communities was family life in Singapore the general pattern.

Up till the 1920s, those Chinese or Indians who did have families in Singapore were mostly well-to-do businessmen and shopkeepers. The upper class comprised those families descended from the Straits-born Chinese businessmen who had come to Singapore from Malacca in the 1820s. From the mid-nineteenth century onwards, there was a small-scale English-educated clerical class to which Singapore Eurasians tended to belong.

EARLY FAMILIES

Families may have been thin on the ground, but the early demography of Singapore had some characteristics highly significant for women. First, they were in short supply, which enabled them or, more likely, their families, to be selective in the choice of marriage partner. Conversations that I overheard between older women speaking of families in their circles suggest that local-born Chinese families tended to favour an enterprising and upwardly mobile young immigrant as a son-in-law. The stereotype was that the local boy was often spoilt and indulged by his "nonya" [Straits-born] mother, whereas the immigrant was hardworking and a good provider. Moreover, by definition, he was here alone; the dreaded mother-in-law was safely tucked away somewhere in China.

Colonial scholar J.D. Vaughan observed Chinese marriage customs in Singapore in the 1860s (see Vaughan [1879] 1971). He describes in detail the negotiations between the bride's parents and the groom, implying that it was a general custom for the groom to arrange his own marriage. Only as an aside, and towards the end of his account, does Vaughan mention that if the groom's parents were in Singapore, then it would be for them to handle arrangements. He makes it clear that this was not the most usual situation. Therefore, in Singapore, things were totally different from customs in China, where marriages were always family-to-family arrangements, with go-betweens very much in the picture.

The traditional role of the ogre mother-in-law in the life of the young wife in China is too well documented to call for comment. In Singapore, the bride was more likely to have the supportive presence of her own mother and kin. Straits Chinese "Peranakan" culture dominated Singapore Chinese society right up until the 1940s, and because she expected to go on living in close contact with her own mother after marriage, the young maiden nonya was rather feared as an uppity bride. For this reason, families with a son sometimes sent off to kin in China to find a China-born and more biddable bride and daughter-in-law. But such was the prestige of Peranakan culture that this bride would also soon be wearing sarong-kebaya and chatting away in the Malay-based patois of her in-laws' household, and she would also have learned to cook in Peranakan style. Several ladies whom I knew personally in the 1950s were in every cultural sense "true-blue Peranakan", although they had been born in China.

Looking at the Report on the Census of Population at the dawn of the twentieth century, the Peranakan were listed separately from the China-born. The Straits-born demonstrated a more or less normal sex ratio, while among the China-born there were getting on for 4,000 men to every 1,000 women.

From the proportion of men and women in these two categories, it is possible to make some rather piquant calculations. For Singapore Chinese of today whose families go back that far, it seems there is a one-in-four chance that the old lady ancestor was Peranakan, but only a one-in-thirty-two chance that Grandpa was also local-born. Many old family photographs illustrate this, with the women in Straits-style clothes but not the men.

ON THE SOCIAL MARGINS

The extreme gender imbalance among the Chinese, consequent on the pattern of male migration, inevitably created a trade in women. Destitute families in Southeast China provided recruiters with their sons to ship abroad as labourers: daughters could be disposed of to traffickers who supplied the brothels in the prospering "South Seas" to which the sons had gone.

These "trades" that exploited men as well as women have been amply documented. Also, everyone knows about the rags-to-riches tales of the "towkay", who arrived initially as a bonded labourer and managed to "make good" along a continuum from prosperous shopkeeper to legendary tycoon.

Less has been said of the unknown and certainly smaller number of women who managed to rise above bonded prostitution to prosperous positions in life. Nineteenth-century Annual Reports of the Chinese Protectorate bewailed one such category, namely the prostitute who rose from the ranks and graduated to the role of trafficker herself. But she did not constitute the whole story (see Warren 1993).

The shortage of women at that time also enabled prostitutes, who were usually regarded as suffering from some social stigma, to marry out of that low status and achieve a family role. Those same Annual Reports refer to very young girls who, by statute, the staff of the Chinese Protector could remove from a brothel to a protective Home, the Po Leung Kuk, built especially for this purpose in the 1880s. From this Home the girls' marriages were arranged (with their consent, we are told) to decent young artisan men who applied to be considered for a wife, as they were not well enough off to seek a wife from any other source.

From prostitute, such a girl rose to the status of wife, but of a humble man with all the struggles that that implies. There are, unfortunately, no after-histories of these arranged marriages, but some of these couples must have prospered in the buoyant colonial economy. One used, occasionally, to encounter a middle-class family member ready to confide (rather sheepishly) that the grandmother of one branch of the family had come from a welfare home, which was likely, in those days, to have been the Po Leung Kuk.

Even without the benefits (and tribulations?) of official protection, some girls rose from the bottom end of the entertainment world to respectable family status. In Singapore as in China, a rich man might fancy a girl from a brothel and take her as a secondary wife. For China, C.K. Yang documents that provided she behaved with decorum, the secondary wife with brothel origins enjoyed whatever status attached to the household of the man who had acquired her (Yang [1959] 1965).

Traffickers sometimes presented a pretty young woman first as a cafe "sing-song" girl and, if she was fortunate, some rich man would choose her as a secondary wife before she was initiated into prostitution. A charming and respected old lady in the outer fringes of my in-laws' kin group had joined the family via this route.

In Singapore as in China, however, the status of a secondary wife was precarious. She could be repudiated without redress. But the girl lifted from abject conditions by such a marriage at least had some hope for herself, and more so for any children she might bear. There is plenty of anecdotal evidence that it was usual for a man to regard his children more or less equally, irrespective of the status of the mother.

As poor men in Singapore stood so little chance of finding a wife, the girl discarded by a rich husband stood a good chance of remarriage to a poorer man, who would value her as a partner for life.

In such cases, the couple would simply set up house together. The fact that they regarded their union as a marriage and were viewed by others as a couple conferred customary marriage status on the arrangement. Right up to the 1961 Women's Charter, such "followed marriages" were among the range of accepted customary unions, and were the refuge of many low-income young people who lacked the kin necessary for a full-scale customary celebration. If one had no family altar to which to make obeisance and no elders around to whom one could serve filial and respectful tea, then there was no way one could celebrate a formal Chinese customary marriage.

Such setting-up-house-together marriages were legal; several court cases confirmed this. But they were socially somewhat "infra-dig". I recall that third parties would lower the voice when pointing out that a certain couple had had only a "followed marriage". In the first year after the passing into law of the Women's Charter, in September 1961, there was something of a rush of middle-aged couples anxious to make sure that their union was, in fact, legal, by registering under the new legislation. They need not, in fact, have worried, but, as one couple said in my presence, they felt better for making quite sure.

The British colonial system ensured that the movement of people between Indian ports and the Straits Settlements, mainly Singapore and Penang, was more regulated than the equivalent movement from China. There is no documented reference to the existence of any trade in women from India. But Leonore Manderson does record, in *Sickness and the State: Health and Illness in Colonial Malaya, 1870–1940* (1996) that there were prostitutes, in smaller numbers, of all ethnic backgrounds in various brothel neighbourhoods in Singapore. James Francis Warren documents, in *Ah-ku and Karayuki-san: Prostitution in Singapore, 1870-1940* (1993), that there was, in the nineteenth century, active trafficking in Japanese prostitutes to all the major urban centres in Southeast Asia.

During the early and mid-nineteenth century, British officials in India regarded Singapore as a convenient place to dump prisoners who were serving long sentences. Among these convicts were a small number of women who, like many of the men, stayed back in Singapore even after completing their sentence.

Many of these convicts were of high caste and their offences were quite often what we would now classify as "social/political activism", but which posed a threat to the colonial power. There is much documentation of the freedom many were allowed in Singapore and of their commendable work record. John Frederick Adolphus McNair and W.D. Bayliss document their skills and diligence in the building of both the Istana and St Andrew's Cathedral (see McNair and Bayliss 1899).

Given the demography of the period, it is not surprising that the women convicts found marriage partners and settled into the family life of the era. In Australia it has, fairly recently, become a source of pride to claim descent from the early convict settlers, but this has so far not happened in Singapore!

What can we know of the quality of women's family life in early Singapore? Regrettably, the answer is not a great deal, but at least some did not lead enclosed lives. Mid-nineteenth-century colonial observers commented that women with children could be seen everywhere in markets, and travelling with their purchases in public conveyance. It can be inferred that daughters of marriageable age were rarely allowed outside the home.

Of special interest is the hard data recorded in the first relatively modern population count, the Report of the 1871 Population Census. Several thousand women were listed as income earners. Depressingly, the largest single category (about 25 per cent) appears as "profession not stated", with a discreet note that these were mostly prostitutes. But this was, by no means, the whole story. There were more dressmakers than domestic servants, and there were mat weavers and basket makers. Some women ran lodging houses, sold cakes or cooked food, or were listed as owning a shop. Nearly as many were listed as fisherwomen as were in domestic service. Refreshingly, 160 women were listed as "planters, managers, overseers". It is tantalising that we will never know what they planted, or whom they managed or oversaw.

A well-documented woman of property of that era (indeed earlier than the 1871 Census), was the redoubtable Hajjah Fatimah (Lee 1990). A wealthy widow in her own right, she employed a British architect and a French contractor when she built the mosque which bears her name to this day and is located at the Kampong Glam end of Beach Road. The records state that she carried on a "large trade" and owned many seagoing vessels. Hurrah for her!

9

The Low-income Family Arrives: Singapore Housing before the HDB "Revolution"

In the 1920s, the decade when low-income families began, for the first time, to settle in Singapore in large numbers, the problem of housing was greatly intensified. But for these newcomers, the squalor in Singapore seemed preferable to the chaos developing in Southeast China (see Wee 1972 and 1996 for more information on this subject).

The last years of imperial China and the period following the Sun Yat Sen Revolution in 1911 was a chaotic time for people living in rural areas. Law and order had broken down, and the villagers lived in constant fear of bandit raids. "I didn't know if I could find work in Singapore, but I knew people there had enough for me to survive by begging. In the village we were all near starvation, there was no one to beg from." This was how an old Cantonese woman, in a Singapore television documentary in 1992, described her decision to leave China in the late 1920s. The colonial economy had its ups and downs but was, by comparison, seen as safe and prosperous.

This was the period when humble men began to revise their life plans of retirement in China, and to bring wives and children from the home village to settle in Singapore. One such artisan placed, over the doorway of his modest Singapore back street home, a traditional signboard, which, in gold characters, told a story of poignant significance for his entire generation. In translation it read, "We brought our rice fields to the South".

As a consequence of all this, the 1920s witnessed a profound, yet seldom referred to, revolution. 1920–30 was the first decade in Singapore's modern history when births outnumbered deaths. Up to that decade, population growth had stemmed from mass in-migration of single adults hence deaths had always far outnumbered births. In the 1920s the Singapore baby "took a bow", and from then on shaped the island's demography.

Singapore was gradually becoming a settled society of families rather than a dormitory town of sojourner men. But Singapore's housing stock was not ready for this transformation. Urban street housing was designed to meet the needs of the business or shopkeeper family, not to house the families of the poor.

The typical Chinatown house had a ground (that is, first) floor for business or retailing and the storage of goods, and above that a floor to provide living space for bachelor employees. From the street, the top floor could be seen to be fronted by a balcony, typically embellished by a ceramic balustrade glazed in green. This was where the owner of the business, the "towkay", and his family enjoyed their airy accommodation, well above the dust and bustle below. Not all businesses sustained a team of live-in workers, and not all houses gloried in an elegant, top floor with a balustrade, but this was a quite commonly found design.

Fortunately, by the early decades of the twentieth century, motor transport transformed the lifestyle of the business owner and his family. They now tended to move away from city-centre housing to bungalow life in suburban areas, such as Katong and Pasir

Panjang. The social—as well as floor—space they vacated was filled in with the ever-increasing number of families of the poor.

The house designed for a business family did not provide ideal accommodation for low-income families struggling to set up home in Singapore. The ground floor usually continued to house business activities but the upper floors became warrens of cubicles, divided and subdivided to accommodate one more couple desperate for a home.

On the second floor the front cubicle had the luxury of a window, or there might be two cubicles wedged into that space. All the other cubicles on that floor lacked direct access to air and natural light. Partitions, usually made of planks, stopped 20–30 centimetres from the ceiling, the space above being filled with chicken wire. Through this wire filtered air and grey daylight, as well as every detail of the private life of those living in the next cubicle.

Even when the inner city was wired for electricity fans were rare, and the chief tenant would not tolerate the switching on of lights before nightfall. The chief tenant would often be living with her family in one cubicle. The rent paid to her included electricity and water. Overuse of the low-wattage bulb which dangled over each cubicle was strictly monitored. The chief tenancy was presumably in the name of the head of the household, the husband, but the "enforcer" was always referred to as a woman.

A *Straits Times* photograph of the early 1950s shows a young boy in school uniform sitting astride a pavement kerb, doing his homework under a streetlamp. Perhaps he had been scolded by the chief tenant for turning on the cubicle bulb too early, or maybe the street seemed more quiet and conducive to homework than the overcrowded conditions upstairs.

Cooking, washing and bathing were carried out in the shared utility space out across the airwell at the back of the main house, provided water was piped as far as the upper floor, which was not always the case. It was not uncommon for ground-floor backyard facilities to serve the needs of two floors of the families living in the cubicles upstairs.

Until near independence, the only sanitation was a shared bucket at the back of the ground floor, replaced early each morning by municipal arrangement. As the desirable bungalow residences in such places as Stevens Road and Balmoral Road had the same bucket sanitation until the early 1950s, there was no particular class distinction in that aspect of Chinatown life. The extreme hardship lay in a number of cubicle dwellers in one Chinatown house all sharing one bucket latrine (see Kaye 1960 for more data on post-War housing conditions and the hardships of shared latrines in tenements). That no epidemic struck Singapore is a tribute to the combination of devotion to personal cleanliness on the part of the population, and the daily diligence of the municipal sanitary squad, who were underpaid and underappreciated.

Given the hardships of inadequate facilities, the general level of cleanliness of the slum families was indeed remarkable. My duties, as part of the Social Welfare Department in 1955–6, involved many home visits to families dwelling in cubicles. While the street-level door was usually left open, once one climbed the stairs—frequently with crumbling wall plaster held in place with gummed newspaper—there was always a locked wooden door made by a carpenter at the top of the stairs. In response to a knock came the opening of a moveable hatch at eye-level, and "multiple eye" inspection to ensure the bona fides of the visitor, by all the cubicle-dwellers who happened to be home at the time. There would be more disintegrating plaster along the upstairs passageway inside the door. But inside the individual cubicles the lino floor covering was spotless, and there was usually a pile of laundered, ironed snow-white school uniforms, as was the universal requirement of all Chinese-language schools of those days.

The emergence of a mass of low-income families in the 1920s and 1930s set a trend for Singapore to represent some of the most grossly overcrowded slum conditions in the world. But from the lifestyle of those I visited, I estimate these were slums of hope. Charles J. Stokes draws a distinction between what he calls "slums of hope" and "slums of despair" (see Stokes 1962). As a student volunteer in the poorest parts of London in the 1940s, I had visited homes where the living conditions were indescribably squalid. On returning home after a visit, it was necessary to stand in the long bath and change clothes to the skin, lest one had brought home fleas or other forms of vermin. Britain had had compulsory education since 1870, and the slum population that I encountered in the 1940s had, for some reason, failed, for several generations, to get their feet onto the running board of upward mobility. These were slums of despair. In contrast, the people of the slums in Singapore had never had much in the way of a chance in life, and as Singapore developed they were ready to use every opportunity to move on and up to a better general standard of living. The personal histories of many older leaders in the public and private sectors illustrates this lifetime trajectory.

The inner-city cubicle was not the only housing resource of the poor. Immigrant families also peopled the island's rural areas, where sizeable Chinese peasant farm communities developed, sometimes in the immediate hinterland of Malay fishing villages. As the city population grew, so did the demand for fish and farm produce, vegetables, pork, eggs and poultry.

Some rural dwellers secured enough land to work up a good income, and in at least one area a division of labour between villages contributed to a comfortable income for all. In one Teochew village at the end of the old Jurong Road, at Tuas, the men worked away from home for weeks at a time, in the highly skilled industry of building and repairing fishing stakes (known locally by the Malay name *kelong*). The women of that village tended to breeding sows and reared litters of piglets only to a size where they could cope with the necessary scrubbing down and general care. The piglets were then sold to a more inland village, where the men worked full-time on rearing these heavier young pigs to marketable size (see Goh 1955).

Some rural dwellers had enough land to yield a good income from vegetables, pigs and poultry. They were able to afford quite comfortable housing, with concrete floors, solid plank walls, wooden louvre windows and stable zinc sheeting roofs. But as the population increased and workable land was taken up, so the number of marginal dwellers increased, with barely a house site, and no access to workable land.

These marginal rural families scraped by mainly on the "odd-job" earnings of the male breadwinner, whose job search was commonly facilitated by an ancient, rusted bicycle. Jobs included mending the often flimsy rural housing, roofs and walls easily damaged by winds, storms or heavy monsoon rain, or unloading heavy sacks which would arrive at the rice shop or perhaps at a building site, or at the quayside of the Singapore River.

These families were too poor to be granted credit at the village general store. What they had to eat for the next twenty-four hours depended on what the father brought home that night, which would perhaps be enough to pay in cash for some rice and oil and a little salted fish. Often, though, the meal would probably have been only rice and soy sauce.

There was evidence that some of these clusters of Chinese rural houses did not get enlarged in a haphazard manner. In my work with the Social Welfare Department, I found, on some rural home visits, that a cluster might comprise families with only one surname. The sprawling shantytown of wooden housing, in the location of the present-day upmarket Henry Park, comprised exclusively families with the surname "Ang". I also encountered a comparable cluster of "Soh" families.

The only possible conclusion to draw from these examples was that one or more families from the same lineage (or "clan") village in China had originally settled in these sites. In the following years, other families from their respective villages had come to join them, and established their housing nearby. In this way, they duplicated the pattern of lineage settlements as was the norm in their provinces of origin in China.

I encountered Soh village in 1951 as a member of a research group organised by the Department of Economics of what was then called the University of Malaya. I was to act as supporter and mentor of one student interviewer, who was given a list of households to visit. Our list included a Soh family living in a squatter area with a lot of open ground, then behind a single row of bungalows along Kheam Hock Road.

In the hope of finding everyone home, we were to visit in the early evening. As we walked across the stretch of rough, open grassland towards the address on our list, we noticed that from every doorway in sight a man was emerging and making his way to the same house. On our arrival, this assembly spoke to the student. We learned they were all also named Soh, and once they were sure that our visit was purely friendly, they gradually sauntered off. They had no interest in what we had come to discuss; their intentions were purely protective, to ensure that we did not represent some possible harm to the family we were visiting. We were impressed that life in a clan village provided rural dwellers with a valuable informal protective social network.

Following up on these discoveries of lineage villages, in 1960, Chang Soo, a Social Welfare Officer on study leave, undertook research to pursue this pattern of surname clustering. He was able to locate numerous examples. Perhaps his most interesting find was the existence of a pair of lineage villages on the site of what has now become the Chai Chee HDB housing area. A Poh village bordered on a Tan village. In the 1920s these two villages had become involved in a "border dispute". The elders of the Poh village told Chang Soo that community leader Tan Kah Kee had influenced officials to give a decision that favoured Tan village. From that time on, the neighbours had not been on speaking terms, and no young Poh woman was permitted to marry any man of the surname Tan.

Another style of congregate living was practised by immigrant men—alone or with family—from Bawean, an island off the Indonesian coast near Surabaya. In Singapore they were commonly referred to as "Boyan", but this is a name that they themselves rejected and disliked. It is said that the Baweanese were more experienced in the care and management of horses than others, and that they first found employment in Singapore in the days of horse-drawn transportation. They were employed as coachmen, and then adapted their skills when motor transport developed. I recall that, in the 1950s, they had almost a monopoly of the occupation of chauffeur to private families.

The care of horses at the Turf Club was also in the hands of Bawean men, and they occupied all the employee quarters there. Many lived in quarters provided by their employers, as was often required of the chauffeurs of well-to-do families in spacious mansions with staff premises out at the back.

The Baweanese also commonly sought the tenancy of a bungalow which had become too run-down for well-to-do occupants, and divided this into small living spaces to accommodate immigrants from only one village. Abdullah Malim Baginda, a Social Welfare Department officer from Kuala Lumpur on study leave at the University in Singapore in the late 1950s, researched the Baweanese community. He found that "house rules" decreed that only cupboards were allowed as room dividers, as these could be moved if the arrival of another family required that space be made to accommodate them.

These were well-structured living arrangements known as *pondok*, which in Malay means a hut but which has wider usage in Indonesian, to include any lodging place (see Baginda 1959 for more details on the Baweanese pondok system). There were accepted rules by which, for example, married families and single men were accommodated on different floors of the house. Each pondok had a headman in charge, known as the *lurah*. This is an Indonesian word for "village headman", but in Malay it does not have that meaning (it can refer to a ravine or a headman). There was even a registered society of these headmen—a Persatuan Lurah Bawean.

Like all others, the pondok-dwelling families later moved into individual HDB flats. I was told recently by someone who spent his childhood in a pondok that, during the Hari Raya season, former pondok residents make a point of inter-visiting, and still feel a special former same-village relationship. I am, unfortunately, not up to date on information regarding the Chinese families who formerly clustered in lineage-based shanty areas nor on what links, if any, they have maintained in the new Singapore.

All these varieties of congregate living—the *kongsi* (singleton dormitory), the lineage village and the pondok—fostered mutual help and social support. But by modern standards they were way below what we can accept in terms of personal space, quality of physical environment and access to facilities such as piped water and modern sanitation.

The years of the Japanese Occupation saw the state of housing deteriorate further. In 1945, the returning colonial government seemed helpless in the face of housing conditions where people were sleeping in bed spaces under the staircases of city tenements, and shacks had sprung up in every urban interstice.

The colonial-era Singapore Improvement Trust, from the 1920s, constructed some very useful lower middle-class housing, but made hardly any inroads in the eradication of slums. In 1959 came partial independence, and in 1960 the setting up of the Housing and Development Board (HDB). Resources and legal powers that were undreamt of in colonial days made it possible for HDB to tackle the problem, first, via the provision of one-room flats with rents only a little above rents for cubicles, and thenceforth via the long road towards the general raising of the standard of living. This strategy has enabled every family forming the mass of the population to, at this point, have a decent-sized home of their own. In Chapter 8, I noted that in Singapore is articulated the notion that the family is the basic building block of society. The achievement of decent homes for all is surely a prerequisite for making this ideal possible.

The eventual outcome is a society with an unusually high proportion of home ownership, which means a population with an unusually high level of familial material assets. But the "social surgery" by which this was achieved involved some adjustments that were painful for many of those involved.

Long-term residence in shantytowns and tenement properties enabled the growth of close social relationships. In the case of lineage villages, these relationships were based on pre-existing neighbourly ancestral ties from the countries from which residents or their parents had come. Even where flat allocation was by balloting, caring HDB officers were said to have informally permitted a certain amount of "swapping" to allow a degree of choice; nonetheless, it was not possible to transpose the old clustering to the new estate.

There were economic costs to the move, especially so for people from rural areas where they had been fortunate to have had space for growing vegetables or rearing poultry or pigs. For them, the move involved a loss of income thus they needed to seek other forms of employment.

Issues related to rent also cropped up. Those who had been living in cubicles at the front of a tenement shophouse and had enjoyed the advantages of a window were already paying a rent comparable to the early rents of one-room flats, but most poorer-quality cubicles had been much cheaper. The higher rent, on moving to a flat, was a burden to those with low earnings.

The move from slum to flat changed the "budget structure" of the family. Payment of rent to the chief tenant had always been fairly flexible. If poverty forced the family to delay payment, relations with the chief tenant might become acerbic and scratchy but eviction was rare. The first call on monthly wages had always been the settlement of the rice shop bill.

For all those rehoused, there were costs seen as intrinsic to the higher standard of the new home. The rough-hewn wooden stools and tables that had served in the passage outside the cubicle "did not look well" (this was the phrase used) in the airy flat. Each family would buy a low table with several vinyl-covered chairs with wooden arms as a minimal needed for decent living in the new home. Where possible they also bought a glass-fronted display cabinet with some china or glass items for the shelves. The cabinet was always placed opposite the front door, so that when it was opened those outside could witness the family's good standing. If a family was able to afford a refrigerator, this was located in the display position, though at this point in time, refrigerators were still somewhat of a luxury.

Residents' Committees and other "grassroots" organisations have been active in seeking to build community togetherness in the new towns, and over the years numerous community organisations have brought residents together for common activities. Over time, new forms of neighbourliness have grown out of the interactions of daily life. Moreover, the generous subsidies available for those seeking a flat in proximity to households with which they are related, have enabled the growth of kin networks of mutual help and support.

10

The Singleton Dormitory: Constructing a Social System in the Absence of Family

"When my elder brother married, my mother drew me aside. We only had land enough for one family, and if I were to marry there'd be no land for me. Therefore she sold the pigs and gave me the money, with the advice that I migrate to Singapore and make a living there. Other men from our village were in Singapore already. My mother had an address on a piece of paper, and told me that with this, any rickshaw puller down at the Singapore port area would know how to take me to where fellow villagers would look after me." These are more or less the exact words, but in a mix of Cantonese, Malay and English, of Mr Lam, a charming elderly contractor whom I happened to be placed next to at a wedding dinner sometime in the 1970s.

Without realising it, Mr Lam was relating the whole story of the massive male migration to the Nanyang which shaped the demography of Singapore from the early nineteenth century until about 1920. The peasant lands of Kwantung and Fukien provinces were becoming grossly overpopulated and very survival required massive out-migration, with the prospering Dutch and British colonial economies in Southeast Asia as obvious destinations.

Mr Lam was one of a fortunate minority who set out for the Nanyang with a modest working capital to pay his way and get started in his new life. I wish I had learned more about his early beginnings in Singapore, but wedding-dinner etiquette hardly allows for anthropological interviews and all I know I learned afterwards, from the bridegroom's brother. This gentleman knew Mr Lam as a prosperous contractor who could be trusted to organise an excellent standard as regards the scrubbing out of the holds of ships at the port. Mr Lam had clearly made good use of that pig money!

Perhaps the Singapore address that Mr Lam's mother had all ready to give him, was of a type of dwelling arrangement which Dr Goh Keng Swee refers to as a kongsi (mentioned in Chapter 9). In his 1953–4 social survey of low-income households in urban areas of Singapore, he found that 12 per cent of "household heads" were single immigrant men, catering alone (that is, buying their own food individually) but sharing living space with others, usually from the same village of origin in China. The kongsi might have been only one cubicle or a whole floor of a shophouse. Some kongsi comprised so many men that they could afford to rent a whole row house for their exclusive use. Dr Goh's information related only to Chinese immigrant dormitories, but I have been told that a very similar pattern existed among immigrant Indian men in the Serangoon Road area.

The kongsi would always include a wooden sleeping platform that ran the length of the room, each resident's sleeping space marked by his rolled-up sleeping mat and bundle of possessions. If the men were in daily employment, they returned to the kongsi after work and used the sleeping space reserved for them. If a man was required to live in at his place of work, then the kongsi was the place he returned to only when he had time off. His sleeping space would be reserved for him, and his bundle of possessions kept safely.

Men also lived there when they were unemployed, between jobs or retired due to old age.

Slum clearance, that began with the founding of the HDB in 1960, led, in respect of one old shophouse, to a search through documents to identify the legal tenant. This was necessary for purposes of compensation. A lawyer described to me how the original tenant was found to be a "Mr Tan Kah", who had been granted tenancy in 1912. Why had it never been handed on? It was virtually inconceivable that this Mr Tan would be still alive. A deeper enquiry suggested that the clerk who had written the original document had probably not been Chinese—he had not realised that there was no such person as this Mr Tan—the tenants comprised, in fact, a "Tan brotherhood".

In Francis Tan's study of several kongsi occupied by Teochew men (see Tan 1963), all were associated in one way or another with the flourishing charcoal trade, then centred around the Beach Road area. One or two of these Teochew kongsi comprised large numbers of men, each renting a whole row house, but in several only a few older men remained. Each kongsi included an altar in honour of the village lineage ancestors. They were all proud that they had been able to arrange for someone to bring, from the altar in their respective home village temples, a small amount of joss ash to place in a jar on the altar in the kongsi, giving what they saw as authenticity to the rites they held in the kongsi.

Although they tended to cater individually, the men in each kongsi comprised an active social group. They spent their leisure time together, often, as Tan notes, reminiscing about life back in their village of origin, and sharing advice on how to cope with diet and other aspects of life in Singapore. If one of the men became unemployed, his kongsi "brothers" would be active in helping him find a new job.

One of the larger kongsi had even organised an unemployment insurance fund into which every man paid a contribution each employed month. Should any man be unemployed for a while, say on account of illness, he could draw, from the fund, enough to meet his basic needs. The banking of this fund and all the accounting was handled by one man, who was regarded as the headman of the kongsi and in whom all the men had complete trust. Interestingly, this kongsi included several men of different surnames from other village lineages, who were related by marriage to someone of the main surname group. These "outsider" men contributed, like everyone else, to the rent, but they were excluded from the insurance fund.

The smaller kongsi had been reduced in size because members had prospered to the point where they could afford to marry and set up a family household. Alternatively these were men who had left their wife and perhaps children back in China, and had prospered to the point of being able to afford to bring the family south to live in Singapore. However, all these former members, who included Tan's own father, continued to contribute towards the rent, and came back for the various annual celebrations at the kongsi "ancestor altar", which often included a modest catered dinner. These kongsi, which had each started out as a dormitory for single men from one specific village lineage, "graduated" to become lineage associations, or what are commonly referred to as "clan associations".

Single male immigrants of several dialect groups organised their lives in Singapore by means of kongsi arrangements. From only one dialect group, the Cantonese, was there sizeable immigration by single women, who also lived in Singapore, mainly in fellow-villager kongsi. The growth of the silk industry in some neighbourhoods of Guangdong province had provided unprecedented opportunities for young women to undertake respectable work outside the domestic circle (Stockard 1989 is a great read on the impact of the silk industry on the lives of women in Guandong). Uniquely in China, this allowed a daughter to bring home as much income as a son. One result was a reduced enthusiasm of families for early marriage arrangements for daughters, and even led to women choosing singlehood for life.

The emergence of rayon in the early twentieth century reduced the profitability of silk production, and many of the independent-minded young Cantonese women moved to undertake factory work in Shanghai. Initially, small numbers of such women also came south to Singapore and Malaya, to work mainly as domestic servants. In the 1930s, with the threat of Japanese aggression in China, large numbers of young women arrived in Singapore. Women from one neighbourhood, the red-hatted Sam Sui (Three Rivers neighbourhood) women, gained a reputation as skilled building labourers. Cantonese women also worked in rubber packing warehouses and as petty street traders, dealing in fresh foodstuff. The largest group, however, were in domestic service.

I had some detailed information about two Cantonese women's kongsi. One comprised only four women sharing a cubicle. Of this group, one woman was elderly and retired, the other three, all in domestic employment, were daughters of her two brothers. In the 1920s, these younger women had been working in factories in Shanghai. By the end of that decade Japan was seen as a threat, and the father of two of the women came personally to Shanghai to persuade them, and their cousin, to return to their home village. When they got home, they found that an aunt, who was already working in Singapore, was home on holiday. When she returned to Singapore she took her three nieces with her and, through her European employer, managed to arrange domestic employment for them. In the 1950s the older woman was supported by her nieces, one of whom had adopted a baby girl and was paying her aunt extra to take care of the child.

The other Cantonese women's kongsi group had rented a small two-storey row house which accommodated fifty-two women. Forty-nine of these women shared the same surname, while three were widows of men of that surname. I was told that this village group was even bigger, and because of overcrowding had rented one floor above a shop around the corner. This shop was owned by a man from their village.

This larger group was said to go back to about 1917. A woman from that village had married a man working in the tin industry somewhere near Ipoh in Malaya. This man had prospered and left his childless widow relatively well provided for. She had returned to the village and persuaded the daughters of several of her brothers to accompany her to Singapore, by paying for their expenses. My informants had no idea why this widow was determined to settle in Singapore nor what connections she already had there. All they knew was that she and her nieces were the original group to settle in this row house.

In the 1950s the working-age women of this larger kongsi were all employed—as were the three younger women from the small kongsi—in what they viewed as the more skilled aspects of domestic employment, working as cooks, or caring for babies and young children. Older women were exempted from rent payment and lived frugally on their savings. They were proud that none of them sought public-assistance allowances. On one occasion when I called at this house, I noticed screens placed halfway across the room, and caught a glimpse of card tables at which sat women who were, by their appearance, not members of the kongsi. My main informant, a retired woman, met me at the door; from her body language, I gathered that on this visit she and I would be chatting out on the "five-foot way" (five-feet wide pedestrian sidewalks projected from the wall of the building into the street) and not inside the house. I sensed my visit should be short and soon made my departure. The older women were, almost certainly, making some income from organised gambling which they well knew to be strictly illegal, and about which the less I knew the better!

When speaking in English, Singaporeans usually used the word "kongsi", as does Goh in his study (Goh 1958). This Hokkien form was much used with several different meanings to refer to a business company, or the title given to clan associations in Penang. For example, the Khoo Kongsi is a fine clan association building, where the artwork is a tourist attraction. In everyday usage, a group of friends going out to lunch together might say "let's kongsi", which would refer to sharing lunch expenses.

In Chinese dialects, these residential arrangements were called "labourers' room". The exception was one less common arrangement, which in the Hokkien dialect was described by a phrase which used one Hokkien term linked to an adjective which was a distortion of the Malay word *tumpang* which means "to lodge", but on a temporary basis. The phrase as spoken was *lompang keng* or "lodging room". This described an arrangement by which the owner or tenant of a whole shophouse carried on a business on the first floor and allowed men from his village to lodge on the second floor. These men might be either working for him or be employed outside, merely living on his premises. The Hokkien informant who described this arrangement claimed that it added to the prestige of the businessman in his community.

Two final-year social work students in the 1970s, Miss Chua Yeok Lung and Miss Lleander Choo, were in a fieldwork placement which brought to light some interesting information regarding single-person living arrangements in the Chinatown area. Their placement was with a staff member of the HDB, who was responsible for arranging for the rehousing of the residents in old and poor-quality Chinatown housing which was marked for demolition.

Besides the factual information which was the focus of the placement, the students orally reported some very interesting impressions. They noted that the men whom they interviewed in kongsi had very low morale and saw themselves as failures, because they had never earned enough to establish their family household. In contrast, the women who were living in kongsi were very proud of their status. They saw themselves as having achieved independence, and as having made a life for themselves without depending on others. For men, the kongsi should have been a temporary stage on the route to achieving householder status. For the women, life in the kongsi style was in itself the achievement.

The two students also had interesting observations about those solitary dwellers who inhabited what were known as "bed spaces". These were usually spaces enclosed in wire netting under the staircases of shophouses. They noted two patterns of personal history among those they interviewed. Some belonged to village lineages that had clustered in centres of population other than Singapore, and to which they had initially travelled. But in the course of their working life they had accompanied an employer who had moved to Singapore, and had worked here for so long that they had lost touch with their fellow villagers in the original place from where they migrated. Illiteracy and the low general use of telephones in their younger days contributed to this loss of contact. When the time came for them to retire, they had no one with whom to share their living arrangements and hence had no choice except to rent a bed space.

In the case of a few men who lived on their own, the students assessed that they might have awkward personal characteristics. They had originally been members of a kongsi but had fallen out with others and had left to live alone. They were anxious to relate to the students long histories of how unreasonable the behaviour of their fellows had been.

All this information was over and above the data collection required for the placement, and must be treated as purely anecdotal. Nonetheless, it arose from several weeks of contact with this population and seems worthy of being treated as oral history.

The kongsi arrangement belonged to the past. It certainly served to preserve a single person from a lonely old age. But it provided such a low standard of comfort and privacy that it is not a style that one can envisage as a solution to the twenty-first century problems of solitary living in post-retirement years (see Wee 1997 for more such details).

11

Loos and Related Topics

We do not usually associate plumbing with the social sciences, so at first encounter *Clean and Decent: The Fascinating History of the Bathroom & the Water Closet, and of Sundry Habits, Fashions & Accessories of the Toilet, Principally in Great Britain, France, & America* by Lawrence Wright comes as something of a surprise. It is an all-embracing study of the history, mechanics and sociology of domestic sanitary engineering and provides a marvel of detail. It is a "jolly good read" on the history of baths, hand basins and water closets (WCs). The fact that it was published back in 1960 in no way detracts from its value.

Wright is an architect interested in structures, which is perhaps why the book does not include anything on the author's personal experience. Also, it misses any mention of such exotica as the hallowed old rural Singapore system, where family, ducks, fish and pigs lived in happy nitrogenous symbiosis with the fish pond and the water hyacinth patch.

I wrote this chapter on the basis of modest personal qualifications on the subject of some premodern systems of human waste disposal. These come from my personal experience of noisome nooks and crannies in 1930s' rural England, combined with recollections of Singapore in the 1950s, that is, some sixty-plus years ago. 1930s' Britain certainly had more WCs per 1,000 people than 1950s' Singapore, but once beyond the reach of main drains and failing the wealth to build and maintain deep-buried, well-sealed and expensive septic pit-tanks, comparisons came out rather in Singapore's favour.

While I was fortunate to enjoy a childhood relatively up to scratch as regards water and drains, I experienced mindboggling alternatives when I was still quite young. An uncle's family lived in a rather rundown but still impressive country mansion, which at first sight appeared far beyond their middle-class means. The good news was that they rented this magnificent, early nineteenth-century pile for a pittance. The titled owner was glad to have someone he knew and trusted in there, to be watchful for leaks in the roof. Moreover, quality of life could be maintained in the mansion by a plentiful supply of low-wage domestic labour from a depressed coal-mining district a short bus ride away.

But there was also bad news. The premises had neither electricity nor piped water. And no, but no, "mod cons", a term which can semantically apply to any aspect of the well-equipped modern dwelling, but which is used almost exclusively to refer to modern waterborne sanitation.

The attractions of this mansion were many, including a vista of a staircase up which you could have driven a pony and cart, if you had one, which my relatives did not. Childhood visits to this mansion were a delight: capacious stables were the territory of pigeon-rearing and motorbike-tinkering older cousins, and the fruit orchards stretched over acres of grassland. A delight until one needed the loo.

An entire ground-floor wing of the house had been left unoccupied and semi-derelict, and at its farthest end was the door to a chamber of horrors. Even before the door was opened, the pungent whiff in the crumbling corridor outside gave an indication of things to come. Over a pit, open to the sky on the outside, stretched a room-long wooden sitting platform perforated with three round holes. These were not intended to foster family togetherness, a natural assumption on the part of an astonished small child, but to enable the pit's cubic capacity to be utilised to the full. Buckets of sand, with scoops for convenient sprinkling, did nothing to reduce the miasmic stench. Indeed they added a hazard, as even the finest patina of sand spilled accidentally on the sitting boards can be extremely painful for five-year old buttocks and thighs.

The contrast between the elegantly proportioned living rooms and this hidden terror at the "ultima Thule" of the west wing was a shock that I felt almost physically, and that led to my wisely evasive action. While the adults were otherwise engaged, the rolling orchards luckily offered many conveniently secluded spots for occasional and discreet visitation.

Later opportunities for play with farm children elsewhere provided me with further education on primitive domestic arrangements. Games of hide-and-seek among picturesque barns and farmyards led to interesting explorations. But alleyways round the back of the farmhouse were soon recognised as no-go areas. Experienced young noses quickly detected methane in concentration strong enough to fire a kiln.

The magnificent ruins of Rievaulx Abbey, Yorkshire, in northern England are sufficiently intact to give some flavour of life in a rich, sheep-rearing, wool-exporting twelfth-century Cistercian monastery. In the middle ages, as many as 700 monks worked and lived the religious life there, among the beautiful wooded slopes of Rye Dale. Beyond the monastery's ruined infirmary are the remains of an immense stone-lined pit which the wall plaque identifies as the "rere-dorter". This is a fine name, but no more than "church-speak": the *Shorter Oxford Dictionary* defines it as "the privy behind a monastery". Seven hundred monks and one rere-dorter? Try not to think about it!

Before the arrival of modern plumbing, our ancestors must have taken for granted an olfactory environment quite different from our expectations today. The movement of European royal and noble families and their retainers between their great houses or castles several times a year makes sense if only to get everyone out of the way, when the cleanout of midden pits took place.

One of the great sources of the strength of ancient Chinese civilisation was an understanding of what is known in science as the "nitrogen cycle". All animal life, including the human being, takes in food, digests what is needed for maintenance and growth and then passes out waste material which, if returned to the soil, replenishes the health of the soil to produce more food. Not all cultures have been aware of this and indeed have been too squeamish about human waste, and sometimes even about animal waste, to facilitate this cyclical process.

Because the rice-growing farming regions of Southeast China understood this cycle, they were able to support a more dense population than any other peasant farming area in the history of the world. The waste produced by the farm family was carefully prepared for use as a fertiliser. I am told that where farms were near a road, a bucket latrine would be sited by that road and passers-by invited to use the facility—the more the better!

The system continued in the early post-war years in Singapore's rural vegetable farms. But the stench which permeated the neighbourhood of farms using this system soon led to regulation, and farmers were forced to find other methods of fertilising their fields. The authorities in the 1950s wisely instituted a system of producing what was sold as "deodorised sludge", which enthusiastic private gardeners were happy to purchase.

As long as Singapore continued to accommodate farms with a fish pond, a version of the nitrogen cycle continued. The farm family's latrine was a hut with a hole in the floor on a platform over the pond. The human waste nourished green plants, the roots of which provided food for fish. The plants, mainly water hyacinth, when ready for harvest, served as fodder for pigs. Voila, a self-sustaining ecosystem! But regrettably not one which could be accommodated in a period of rapid urbanisation.

Fortunately civil engineering has made many advances since then, but in 1950 I was told that, for much of Singapore, a main drains sewage system was not possible because the "water table" was too near the surface. The municipal alternative was a bucket latrine system. Every day of the week, in the dawn hours, a "32-door wagon" drove around the municipal area. While setting out, each door of the wagon contained a large, oval empty bucket. As the wagon drove by, the labourers travelling with it took an empty bucket to the designated back premises of each house, removed a full bucket and replaced it with an empty one.

Where there were individual family homes, for example, the bungalows in such neighbourhoods as Stevens and Balmoral roads, this was a not-exactly-pleasant but quite tolerable system. And in this case, I speak from personal experience. But in tenement areas such as Upper Nanking Street, where many families who dwelt in cubicles shared one latrine, there was real hardship.

From about 1952 onwards, the sector of civil engineering attained new achievements, and the municipal areas were served by an ever-spreading system of main drains. But in rural areas a variety of alternatives lingered for some years. Only the HDB's momentous rehousing strategies of the 1960s made access to waterborne sanitation a taken-for-granted amenity.

For most, this was a welcome aspect of the rehousing programme. But for some former rural residents, it was a modern amenity of which they were, at first, somewhat circumspect. If one has grown accustomed to a (let's be honest) somewhat "stinky-poo" arrangement, well, outside the living quarters, to learn that in the new housing everything is inside the home, can be, at first, distressing. This was, however, soon overcome by the conveniences of the new home. But I can recall conversations in which my attempts at reassurance regarding the future home completely failed to convince my so-far-rural-dwelling listeners.

In line with the prevailing customs, the HDB provided squat-type sanitary installations, which represent what is believed to be a healthy lifestyle, and were in line with long-established Asian personal domestic habits. In the twenty-first century, the global spread of western fashion coupled with an aging population with knee-joint problems that preclude squatting, have brought in an increasing preference for pedestal-type installations. Indeed, by the 1980s, even the HDB was changing the toilets, making pedestal WCs the standard equipment for new flats.

Public amenities in shopping malls and places of entertainment tend wisely to include one squat-type toilet. But, and here I can speak only of the women's restroom, when there is a rush period, this is virtually always the last cubicle to be occupied.

In 2010, a group of tertiary-level female students from Singapore visited a sister institution in another ASEAN country, and were accommodated in that institution's residential college. Many warm memories and friendships grew from this visit. But not all was sweetness and light. The Singapore staff-in-charge of the visit described, with much humour, the Singapore students' traumatised reactions when they learned that in the shower rooms of the residential college, all toilets were the squat type. In the words of a staff member, "From their shocked facial expressions one would have thought rigor mortis was about to set in!"

Because of its superior hygiene as well as the added benefit of muscular superiority for all but aging and frail knees, we may well live to witness a resurgence of the squat "loo". Meanwhile, the wheel of progress turns and it's knees-up twenty-first century!

Somehow it does not seem quite right to finish on this light-hearted note. Enjoying the luxury of fussing about the style of our modern sanitation, it behooves us to remember that we belong to a privileged sector of humankind. According to United Nations calculations there are still around 2.5 billion people in developing and, especially, rural societies, who do not have access to acceptable forms of sanitation. Of this number, some 1.1 billion lack any facility whatsoever within the secure bounds of the domestic domain. Being compelled to resort to wasteland outside the homestead is not only unpleasant and beneath human dignity, but adds greatly to the vulnerability of women and girls.

We can be proud that Singapore, which initiated the concept of "Sanitation for All" at the UN, also, in 2013, proposed, with the support of 120 national representatives, that 19 November should be designated World Toilet Day. The resolution was passed by consensus, displaying the general recognition that this apparently niche need could "achieve disproportionate and positive outcomes, in terms of health, gender equality, and personal dignity"(Chua 2015). The governments and noble international NGOs that focus on improving sanitation arrangements in the less-developed world certainly merit our support.

12

Names: Fifty Shades of Getting Messed Around

When illiteracy meets bureaucracy, clear the decks. Amazing things can happen.

Like everyone else in Singapore in 1948, Cantonese *amah* Madam Fok Ah Fong, who had had no formal schooling, registered for an identity card (IC). It was only in 1955, when the Central Provident Fund became law, that her employer needed to see her IC in order to complete the necessary forms. "Wah Ah Fong," he read out, that being the name on the IC. Taken aback, Madam Fok screeched in her best high-dudgeon Cantonese, "That is not my name!"

Much discussion followed. The employer guessed that she had been interviewed in 1948 by a Hokkien-speaking clerk whose use of language had confused Madam Fok into thinking he was asking for her personal name, when he was in fact asking for her full name. Trying to use Hokkien herself, she had replied, "Wah Ah Fong" which means (in Hokkien), "I am Ah Fong". A statutory declaration enabled by her employer restored Madam Fok to her rightful identity.

87

A somewhat comparable problem, stemming from misunderstanding in a question–answer situation, led to the misnaming of a Singaporean Malay man. All his brothers carry their father's name, as is customary: they were all "bin Osman". But this man's documents showed him to be "bin Apa". During his birth registration, the Malay-speaking clerk had asked the mother for the father's name. As there was a lot of noise at that time the mother did not hear what was said and, asking the clerk to repeat the question, she used the appropriate Malay word, "Apa?" For some reason the clerk mistook this question for the answer, and filled this in as the father's name.

Three generations back, a baby boy of the Fan family was somehow registered with the surname "Wham" on his birth certificate. As no dialect surname exists which corresponds anywhere close to this Romanisation, one can only conclude that on this occasion Chinese illiteracy was attended to by non-Chinese bureaucracy. But Wham this person remained, and so has his family; no doubt, the several Whams in the telephone directory are his descendents.

An acquaintance informed me that her elder sister was born soon after her parents arrived in Singapore from China sometime in the 1960s. Her father sought to register her sister's birth, and chose for the baby a personal name not in common use in Singapore at that time. The clerk at the registry asked the father how this name should be spelt in English alphabet. Educated only in Chinese, the father was unable to make this change from character to Romanised script. The clerk then suggested the father choose "a simpler name", presumably meaning a name in common Singapore usage. Confused by the whole process, the father was unable to oblige. Perhaps meaning to be helpful, the clerk then suggested, "Lily is a pretty name for a girl." Anxious to complete the bureaucratic requirements, the father felt constrained to agree. Known in social and everyday situations by the name her family had first chosen, this lady has otherwise remained Lily whenever confronted with legal documents.

A more common problem arose when a Chinese baby's birth was registered before the family had decided on a personal name. Common sense should have whispered in bureaucracy's ear: "Give them a reference number on a piece of office notepaper and say you will hold the partial registration for two weeks while they buck up and decide on the kiddo's personal name." But as has happened so often in history, common sense was out to lunch. In these instances, the clerk just went ahead and entered "Baby" in the space for the personal name on the registration form. From then on, whatever name the family later chose was only for informal use: for legal purposes the man or woman remained "Baby" for life, even when applying for admission to an old-age home.

This was bad enough even with common surnames with neutral meanings, for example Tan or Lee, but a "Baby" surnamed Pea or Poo was doubly unfortunate. Some decades ago, in a public notice in the local press, in a list of those who had reported a loss of share certificates, there was indeed one Madam Baby Pea.

The Bong family undoubtedly chose a suitable name for their baby boy, but too late for it to be recognised as his official name. In the early 1970s, the son had grown up to be a respected police officer and was required to take the witness stand in a juvenile court case on a day when I happened to be present. As is the case for all witnesses, Inspector Bong had to state his full name and the magistrate had to write it down in long hand, along with all other proceedings. "Detective Inspector Baby Bong, your Honour," stated the witness, a tall, well-built man in early middle age. The juvenile court, at that date, was housed in a temporary premises without air-conditioning, and the noise of traffic in the street outside was quite loud. The magistrate apparently could not believe he had heard correctly and asked the witness to repeat his name, not once but twice. Finally, with obvious embarrassment, the witness called out very loudly "B-A-B-Y Bong, your Honour." "Ah, yes,

yes," responded the rather flustered magistrate, as if apologising. But a painful titter went around the court and I could not but feel that, in this case, bureaucracy had inflicted a painful lifelong wound.

In situations involving migration—which were frequent—where members of the Chinese ideographic culture met Romanised bureaucracy, creativity knew no bounds. In the days of massive Chinese migration to Southeast Asia, when Hokkien-speaking migrants of the Huang clan reached what was then the Dutch East Indies, their surname was recorded as "Oei". If they landed, instead, in Singapore, it became "Wee" and if in Penang, "Ooi". It is noteworthy that even though then British colonial Singapore and Penang were both administratively parts of the Straits Settlements, the bureaucrats never bothered to standardise the recording of Chinese names. Penang had a partiality for the letter "h", so the Chias, Teos and Yeos of Singapore were the "Cheahs", "Teohs" and "Yeohs" of Penang.

On 5 December 2015, the *Straits Times* obituaries recorded the passing of a ninety-five-year-old lady. The names of her late husband, their children and of her husband's siblings were also listed. It is reasonable to assume that all these people have the same surname, but five versions of the name are recorded: Oo, Boo, Woo, Voo and Oh. These are not "fifty shades", of course, but five versions of the same name in one family is pretty wild!

The Chinese were not the only ones to suffer from name mangling. I recall a young Malay man whose parents had clearly intended that his name should be Rosli. Whoever registered his birth apparently encountered a non-Malay counter clerk who was ignorant of Malay culture. As a result, the young man grew up with the name Rose Lee. His name must have led to much teasing at school especially as, in his era, this was the stage name of a Chinese dancer known for her daring performances.

In the course of migration from China to the sugar-growing colony of British Guiana (BG) (now Guyana) in South America in the nineteenth century, naming got really wild. The voyage by ship was very long, and great care was taken to ensure that the migrants survived the three or more months at sea. This care included the selection of men who were literate (earlier, "cargoes" of barracoon-type labourers had mostly died during the voyage). Women were recruited for light estate work in the hope that their presence would lead to marriages and thereby the establishment of a stable Chinese community, an objective which was achieved.

On every immigrant ship there was also an Anglican missionary on board. In 1862 Mr Ho Ah Hing left China, but Mr Andrew Hunter Hoahing arrived at his South American destination. His Chinese names had been run together and he had been baptised en route and given a Christian name, to which was attached the surname of the sugar plantation owner who was paying for his passage and to whom he was therefore bonded in return. The addition of this name made sorting out on arrival much easier. Guyana Chinese of that generation of migrants mostly had their family and personal names run together, creating three-syllable family names, for example Cheeatow and Fungafat.

This is reminiscent of the hordes of migrants from poor areas in Europe to the United States in the early years of the twentieth century. They were processed into the USA via the bureaucracy on Ellis Island in New York harbour. In many instances the children of these migrants, having benefited from the school system of their new country, were motivated to research their family's roots. They often discovered that the family's identity had undergone a veritable sea change on the voyage out.

But back to Guyana, where the population is predominantly Afro-Caribbean and South Asian, with the Chinese constituting no more than a small minority. Within a generation of this demography the Chinese became almost exclusively English-speaking, and lost not only their language but even the skill in pronouncing Chinese names: for instance, Mr Ng-Yeow became, orally, Mr Nig-Yeow.

The story of Mr Andrew Hunter Hoahing had a positive ending. Although he arrived as a credit-ticket immigrant, a bonded labourer on Mr Hunter's sugar estate, the two men developed a relationship of mutual trust and respect. Mr Hunter promoted his labourer to supervisor status, and later helped him start a shop which grew into a prosperous business.

By 1912, Mr Hoahing had two sons studying in London to become lawyers, and a daughter at Edinburgh Medical School. In honour of his erstwhile employer, Mr Hoahing gave all his twelve children the middle name Hunter.

The twelfth child, a beloved and beautiful baby girl, Rachel Hunter Hoahing, was born in Hong Kong when her parents were making a once-in-a-lifetime sentimental visit to their homeland. This baby girl grew up to be my mother-in-law, but that's another story.

13

Adoption: Some Highways and Byways

From the passing into law of the 1949 Adoption Ordinance, there was a legal highway to adoption available. However many people continued to prefer a long established byway (in 1949, Singapore was still a colony, and the official label of all legislation was "Ordinance". Only when Singapore achieved the status of an independent nation were we entitled to call our statutes "Acts").

Cheng Lin's birth certificate, like anyone else's, was a piece of paper. But when at age fourteen she held it in her hand for the first time at school, it struck her like a bolt of lightning and tripped all the switches of her normal functioning.

Her father's name was okay, but in the space for "mother" was the name of a woman she had never heard of. Cheng Lin reeled internally for days, and then the awful truth dawned upon her. Clearly her father had kept a mistress in the past; this did not somehow seem to be her dad's style, but what else could it be? And her dad had pressured her mum to take the mistress' child to rear as her own. Ghastly thought! No wonder her mum was scratchy at times.

Weighted down by this frightful revelation of her origins, Cheng

Lin struggled along like a thundercloud, hating everything and everybody. Her father and mother also struggled on, mistakenly thinking that they were being treated to an almighty dose of teenage hormones. Then, on an especially provocative occasion, the cloud burst and Cheng Lin flung at them the shameful theory of her beginnings. This time it was her parents at whom lightning struck: that they were flabbergasted would be an understatement.

Yes, her father confessed, they had failed to tell her the truth: she was adopted. No birth child could have been more loved, and they saw their failure to tell her the true story as a symbol of how unimportant her being adopted was to them. (This reason for secrecy has often been repeated by adoptive parents in Singapore, although child welfare professionals now advise disclosure at an early age.) The woman named on Cheng Lin's birth certificate was indeed her birth mother but neither her father nor her mother knew her personally, and had met her only once. After years of yearning for children of their own, Cheng Lin's parents had been introduced to Madam Tan, a qualified midwife. This was around 1951, and many women, especially those who were illiterate (as many were), preferred home birth, attended by a midwife of their own dialect group, to the option of registering to give birth at KK Women's and Children's Hospital. Because of their work, often with poor mothers, midwives tended to know of babies who were going to be given away and were, on this account, from time to time approached by those seeking to adopt.

It so happened that Madam Tan did know of a recently born and healthy baby girl who was available. Her birth parents already had four daughters, and had decided they must give away the next born if this baby was not the son for whom they were longing. At the time of birth there were no potential adopters in the wings so, in taking the first steps to register the baby for the issue of that essential document, a birth certificate, Madam Tan had filled in the mother's name. As the husband was working away at sea, she was awaiting his return to copy his name accurately from his identity card.

Madam Tan suggested that as Cheng Lin's mum and dad would like to have the baby, why not fill in her dad's name in the space for "father"? Nowadays we would respond that there was a very good reason for not filling in the father's name in this manner: it was (and still is) illegal, under Section 177 of the Penal Code, to make a false statement on a legal document. But the idea, at the time, seemed entirely sensible to all three concerned—Cheng Lin's dad, mum and Madam Tan. No doubt, if they had consulted the birth mother she would have readily agreed. The birth certificate with Cheng Lin's dad's name, along with his identity card details, would be all that would ever be needed for such formalities as registering for school and so on in the future. Provided that the father's name was in order, no official was likely to bother about the mother's name.

So, as if by magic, Cheng Lin's parents now had a beautiful baby bureaucratically registered as born to them without the hassle and expense of lawyers and courts. Her father paid Madam Tan a fee for attending to the birth mother, as was usual in the circumstances. Madam Tan, well versed in tradition, guided the new parents on the details of the gifts that it was customary to provide for the birth mother in gratitude for her expenses and pain during her pregnancy and delivery. These included two bottles of brandy, a pair of chickens (in those days still a luxury food), some other items such as a length of cloth and a carefully calculated "red packet", cash, but strictly for out-of-pocket expenses and a "thank you" gift, which was in no way to be seen as "buying" the baby.

That fateful family day, when the truth of Cheng Lin's birth came out, and by the time her parents (but mainly her father) had stumbled through a summary version of the story, all three were deeply moved and "there wasn't a dry eye in the house", as used to be said of cinemas when an especially poignant movie was shown.

Cheng Lin was greatly relieved, and her old self more or less returned. But she was now more serious and reflective; in quiet moments, especially in bed, she thought wistfully about her birth mother, and even more about her four elder sisters whom she would never know. These thoughts did not hamper her life in any way, though they never quite went away.

The adoption arranged by the midwife was not uncommon until perhaps about 1970. In my discussions with retired midwives as to their role in the "extra-judicial" placement of babies, they were quite unconcerned about the illegality of what they had done. Indeed, they saw themselves as acting from a moral high ground of saving the adoptive parents much expense and inconvenience.

Moreover, the midwives assured anonymity for the adoptive parents and the child. Until a wise 1970s amendment to the 1949 legislation, legally adopted children were issued with an adoption certificate to replace their birth certificate, which caused some embarrassment in bureaucratic encounters. From the 1970s' amendment onwards adopted children were issued a new birth certificate, which recorded legally the fiction that they had been born to their adoptive parents. Only the Registrar of Births could tell from a code number that this was a duplicate document. This humane amendment provided for retrospective action: anyone with an adoption certificate could apply to have it replaced by a birth certificate.

The retired midwives were emphatic that they had always been careful to accept only adopters who could offer a good family life to the child. They were proud to claim that they had had no truck with any woman whom they suspected to be involved in prostitution, and who might be seeking adopted daughters to rear in her profession. If occasionally a birth certificate labelled a visibly Chinese girl as the birth child of a Tamil or Malay couple, they saw that as a small matter. Both these communities were known to value daughters and to treat them well, so many Chinese birth mothers were happy to think of their baby girls growing up in Malay or Indian families.

Sometimes the role of the midwife was even further extended. In the early 1950s, at least one Singapore couple arranged to adopt a baby born in a town in then still colonial Malaya. A midwife in that town who ran the small private maternity home where the baby was born, arranged for a Singapore midwife friend to complete a Singapore birth certificate, listing the Singapore couple as the birth parents. Armed with this, the couple went north and collected the little daughter they longed for.

There was, in those days, no immigration border between Singapore and the Peninsular. But this was a family who took holidays overseas, and a person born in Singapore was a British subject, entitled to a British passport, while anyone born in the Malay states could hold only the passport of a "British Protected Person". A friend of the writer, born in still colonial Kuala Lumpur, once described the checkpoint delays he experienced because of his lesser known passport, when as a vacationing Cambridge undergraduate he travelled between countries in Europe.

Midwives such as Madam Tan were different in their training from midwives in Singapore today. Nowadays midwifery is a post-basic course, available only to those who are already state-registered nurses. In the immediate post-War period, when the birth rate in Singapore was high, the colonial government recognised the urgency for births to be attended by someone who understood the basics; fully qualified nurses were in much too short supply. To meet the need, women with "Standard 7" education (Secondary 2 or 3 of today) were offered training in the basics of aseptic delivery, together with skills to recognise symptoms that indicated they must bundle the mother into a taxi and get her urgently to KK Women's and Children's Hospital. Many of these midwives practised from their own humble city and suburban homes. In many places one saw a signboard advertising their services, and they did much good work.

Those were times when few uneducated couples knew anything about contraception, and the giving away of surplus babies whom they felt unable to rear was the "family-planning method of the poor". Adoption literature from Western countries seems to take for granted that giving up for adoption was mainly the resort of unmarried and unsupported mothers, that is, women with no regular partner, not those in long-term unmarried relationships (the information about adoptions in Britain is from Kellmer Pringle et al. 1966). In contrast, most of the babies given away in Singapore and Malaya were born to married couples.

The stereotype is that couples gave away only surplus daughters; numerically, for the most part, that was true. But in some cases of very large families, boys also were given away. Two childless couples known to me (but totally unknown to each other and decades apart in age) were in touch with doctors. It so happened that each of these doctors was attending to a pregnant patient where the birth couple had decided that they could not afford another child, be it a boy or a girl. The potential adopters had to agree that, whatever sex, they would accept the expected baby.

Through these contacts each couple finished with two sons, although both would have liked to have a daughter. These boys were all legally adopted via the procedures of the adoption legislation. In each case the adoptions worked out very well, and because of these arrangements four fine graduates are now contributing to society.

But the adoption of boys can involve some complications which are less likely to occur when girls are given away. A cohort study of 11,000 babies born in England in one week in 1946 was continued until these babies reached the age of twenty-five. This permitted a series of quantitative research projects which provided unusually reliable results.

When the cohort was aged seven, the progress of those adopted was compared with that of children reared by unsupported birth mothers. Adopted girls did better, whether they were given away to families of relatively high or low socio-economic status. Boys did better only if adopted by relatively low-status families. Those adopted by high-status families did not do as well, on an average, than those who remained with the birth mother. There was no evidence of why this was so, but the researchers speculated that high-status families perhaps had expectations of their sons that adopted boys were not always able to fulfil. The data comprises an average, of course, and individual cases could show quite different outcomes.

In the 1960s, the writer was active in an adoption sub-committee of the Singapore Children's Society. Membership of this group included several organisations in touch with available babies and would-be adopters. The main source of available babies was the medical social worker from KK Women's and Children's Hospital.

In those days, there were many more Chinese babies available than there were Chinese couples seeking to adopt. There were usually a number of non-Chinese couples, including members of the British forces stationed in Singapore, looking for a daughter. The Children's Society made available one very senior and experienced social worker to visit and work with families seeking to adopt. Where an adoption would involve a little girl growing up in a family of a different ethnic group, great care was taken to ensure, as far as possible, that the potential adopters understood the long-term implications of this and were prepared for the challenges of making the adoption comfortable for all concerned.

There was unfortunately no institutional arrangement by which we could follow up, either to offer support or measure the success of the outcome. In one instance a young woman in her late twenties, Chinese-Singaporean by birth but brought up in England by a British family, did visit a sub-committee member in Singapore. She held a senior technical post and was travelling in connection with her employment in a multinational company. Over lunch she seemed very comfortable talking about her adoption, and gave every indication of being warmly integrated into her adoptive family. She did not recollect any problems and was able to chuckle about being treated as "interesting" and "exotic" at school. On some reflection, she declined the offer of help to find her birth family. "Maybe someday," was her response. One bird does not make a summer, as the old British saying goes, and we have no information whatsoever on the outcome of other such adoptions.

In the experience of that sub-committee, only rarely was a Chinese baby boy available. Perhaps surprisingly, it was much more difficult to find couples to adopt these baby boys. We learned that for a Chinese family, adopting a son was quite different from adopting a daughter.

If a couple took a fancy to a baby girl that was enough, but when they viewed a baby boy that was only the first stage. Grandparents or other members of the extended adopting family would be brought to view the child. The length of his earlobes was commented on, as in folk belief this is an indicator of a boy's potential for longevity. The poor little chap would also have his genitals carefully inspected for any sign of potential generative inadequacy—at the age of one month or so!

Given the Chinese concept of family as a male-descent lineage or clan, there was a logic to all this. A girl, whether she was a child by birth or adopted, was seen as only a sojourner in the family. She had no long-term role in their family, but was married out and had permanence or became a potential ancestor in her husband's family or lineage. A boy, on the other hand, would be a permanent member of the family, a lifelong link in the lineage, so the family would need to be careful in making that choice in the case of an adopted son.

These traditional beliefs have largely disappeared from Chinese family life. From the 1970s, couples have used modern contraceptive methods to regulate family size. The adoption sub-committee was no longer needed in the new situation and was dissolved.

Most of what is written above referred to Singapore and Malaysian Chinese customs. It seemed that only Chinese families regulated their size and the standard of living they could cope with by offloading surplus fertility via the route of giving away newborn babies in adoption. Malay couples with more children than they could cope with turned to the kin group for help, and the long-term fostering of the children of poor relations was quite a common practice. Poor Indian couples seemed to cope somehow, and there was no common practice of giving away of Indian babies.

These patterns of family custom came alive when Indian and Malay childless couples sought Chinese babies to adopt. For them, this cross-cultural arrangement had many advantages. When a Chinese couple gave away a baby they accepted this as final, and did not expect any further contact with the child or the adoptive parents. Both Indian and Malay interviewees expected that the birth parents would later on feel a longing for their child, *rindu* in Malay, a word that expresses a powerful emotion. So there would always be a risk of the birth parents turning up, at best to disturb the adoption, at worst seeking the return of the child.

For Indian Hindu parents, the culture of caste was also a complication. If the child was born of their relatives (same caste), they countered the risk of future interference, and if the child was born of strangers, then marriage in the future might be difficult as gossipmongers would spread rumours that the child must be of a low caste to have been given away.

But low caste was not the only problem. A friend spoke of a childless couple among her relatives in India who had been given a baby to adopt by the officials of a large Mumbai hospital. Being professionals, with a stable marriage and good income, they were viewed by the hospital as suitable adopters for this orphaned baby girl. Everyone was delighted until the couple took the baby to visit their relatives in their ancestral village. The relatives were horror-struck. They, like the couple, were members of a ritually clean agricultural caste, but the baby was Brahmin! By including the baby in their non-Brahmin lifestyle they would all be guilty of some unforgivable Hindu transgression, with terrible consequences for their reincarnation. The adoptive parents were, fortunately, modern-minded, and were part of mainly a metropolitan professional and social circle where tradition was less important.

One of the Chinese baby's great advantages for the Hindu family was her being outside the caste system. Besides, she had a much valued "wheatish" complexion, associated with high social status in Indian culture. Even a casual observation of local social circles indicates that in Malay and Indian communities, Chinese adopted daughters have been acceptable as brides in families of respectable social standing.

I have used the past tense here with good reason. Now that family planning is widely understood and accepted, babies are rarely available for adoption. Indeed, local couples seeking to adopt have been forced to look overseas.

14

Ambushed by the Indian National Army

One day in 1958 an Indian lady-activist, returning from a conference, stepped off a plane in Singapore and announced to the assembled press: "Singapore is one big brothel." The paparazzi lapped this up, but the pro-consular rearguard of that era was not amused.

In the frantic scuttling of damage control, the establishment should have taken comfort that the great Mrs Shirin Fozdar (for the lady activist was none other than she) had been socialised in the Gandhian philosophy of non-violence, and had come from India to settle in Singapore.

Some fifteen years earlier, in 1943, in Japanese-occupied Singapore, another Indian lady activist, inspired by the militant and charismatic Subhas Chandra Bose, had raised an anti-colonial women's regiment trained in the use of firearms and hand grenades. Accusations of brothel tolerance may wound official dignity but are preferable to a well-aimed bayonet below the ribs.

Given to headline catching, as illustrated above, Mrs Fozdar's name became well-known in Singapore; she is revered for her good work to this day, especially among women's civic groups. In contrast, the name of Dr Lakshmi Swaminadhan is almost unknown to Singaporeans. In 1943, as part of the Indian National Army's (INA) plan to fight for the independence of India, at the Burma (now Myanmar) border, Dr Lakshmi raised the Rani of Jhansi regiment. This comprised women recruits from both Singapore and also from Malaya (now Malaysia). There were, in total, some 500-plus dedicated young Indian women volunteers in the regiment, who lived in camp and received training in Singapore in the arts of war.

Joyce C. Lebra brings the "ranis" within the range of the general reader in her book *Women against the Raj: The Rani of Jhansi Regiment* (2008). This can hopefully generate general interest in martial Singaporean and Malayan Indian women, and those stirring times. This is a truly remarkable book on several counts. The author's scholarship is formidable and her theme a serious one, but like the best of serious books this is also "a jolly good read". Radical patriotism and selfless courage in the face of death are virtues we conventionally associate with a male hero. Such tales are the more electrifying when those involved are women, moreover women whose ancestral culture stereotypically restricted them to submissive and domestic roles.

The history of India includes numerous examples of heroic patriotism on the part of women. Perhaps the most notable example was a young equestrian warrior queen of the 1850s who led the earliest major uprising for Indian independence from British colonial rule. She was the original Rani of Jhansi, galloping across the plains of north India, guns in both hands: mown down in battle when barely out of her teens. "The best and bravest of the rebels" was a tribute to her from her British enemy.

In the 1940s, Singapore and Malayan Indian girls, ranging from those of upper-class background to rubber tappers' daughters, volunteered under the banner of this same Rani for the INA military service. They were camped in Singapore's (then) St Joseph's Institution playing fields on Bras Basah Road, from whence they came daily, marching in smart order, uniformed and armed. They were preparing to fight and, if necessary, to die, in a longed for Burmese/Indian border struggle, to free the homeland of their ancestors from British colonial rule.

Lebra's qualifications to write on her chosen field are truly outstanding. It is rare for a history to be written by someone who, along with scholarly documentary research, has held extensive and repeated discussions with so wide a range of the people involved in a historic event.

In her early research on the INA, in the years immediately after the end of World War II, Lebra visited Southeast Asia, India and Japan. The memories of the military leaders of both sides of the conflict were, at that time, still fresh. In *From My Bones: Memoirs of Col. Gurbaksh Singh Dhillon* (1998), G.S. Dhillon writes about the INA, paying warm tribute to Lebra for motivating him to settle down to write. Clearly, Lebra's interviews as well as data collection for her own work were inspirational to others.

Lebra made repeat visits to Asia in 2007 and, in Kanpur, India, was able to once again interview the redoubtable commanding officer of the Rani of Jhansi regiment, Dr Lakshmi Swaminadhan. At the age of ninety-seven, this lady was still attending to patients in her medical clinic and, as recently as 2002, made one more fine symbolic battle gesture—she stood as a candidate for the presidency of India. Did she think she had a chance of winning? No, but it was an opportunity to bring the memory of the INA once more into public view.

In 1945–6, the sacrifices of the men and women of the INA and the Rani of Jhansi regiment to free India, galvanised the Indian masses to a frenzy of patriotic zeal and gratitude that shook the Raj to the roots. Defeated by the British in the 1944 battles on the frontier between Burma and India, what Hugh Toye so aptly describes as the INA's "thunderous disintegration" (Toye 1959: 175) did indeed hasten the day of independence.

As a sad postscript, once India had achieved independence, these same sacrifices were accorded but scant official recognition by the ranks of Indian Congress party leadership. Although Bose had died in 1945, these leaders saw INA officers as competition for the acclaim of the masses. For example, not one of the INA officer corps was offered a rank in the post-independence Indian Army. The valiant Colonel Dhillon, who suffered painful and life-threatening experiences on the Burma border battle front, was reduced to begging the authorities for a taxi-driving licence. Recorded elsewhere is the irony that the only INA veteran offered even a minor diplomatic posting, Colonel Stacey, was the single Eurasian in Bose's inner officer circle. His ethnicity made him a political non-threat to the Congress party elite.

A copy of Manmohan Kaur's *Women in India's Freedom Struggle* ([1985] 1992) is available at the National University of Singapore Library in its third edition, evidence that it has been widely read, perhaps primarily by students of history and women's studies in India. In describing the overwhelming defeat of the Japanese/INA force on the India–Burma border in 1944, this book records that Bose "ordered that the Rani of Jhansi regiment be disbanded and the members sent to their homes" (ibid.: 230).

The reader can almost hear Bose barking an order, "Get the girls on the next train out," which is an unforgivable and mendacious distortion of what really happened. Indian female readers of the editions of this otherwise informative source have been allowed no glimpse of their INA-retreating sisters' "twenty-six day epic of slogging through the jungles of Burma and Thailand, mostly on foot and at night, without food or a chance to bathe" (Lebra 2008: 93). At some points they were out of their depth in rivers, to get across which there were no ferries, and were hauled across by rope. They were forced to fight back when attacked by guerillas, and two girls were shot and killed. They trudged parallel with the retreating INA men, Bose slogging alongside and in command.

As Dr Lakshmi remained in Burma throughout this trek in retreat, the commanding officer of the Rani of Jhansi regiment was a strong and intelligent seventeen-year-old from an upper-class

Kuala Lumpur family. For her, life would never be the same again. She carried this traumatic early experience of military command through a string of business and civic leadership roles in her later life. I had the honour of meeting her in her old age. She was then firm in asserting that she could never have achieved this most creditable record had it not been for her early leadership responsibility in the INA, which toughened her up.

Their service in the regiment gave all "ranis" an educational and maturing experience that would leave them changed forever. Those of the officer corps who continued on more conventional educational tracks after 1945 did indeed go on to be among the outstanding Malayan women of their generation.

Lebra records also her 2007 Malaysian contact with the now elderly mothers and grandmothers who, after the war, returned to their rubber-estate families and filled the conventional roles expected of them. They had pride in their memories, and the pride of their children and grandchildren in their sacrifice for a noble cause. Was this a sufficient follow-up in life for all of them? I had the privilege of a personal experience to suggest that this was sadly not always so, and stemming from this, Lebra's book holds a very special meaning for me.

In 1956, when Singapore was still a colony, in my youthful ignorance I walked straight into an ambush and wham, the Rani of Jhansi regiment struck good and hard, hitting with all the moral force of that inspired women's movement.

As a then staff member of the Singapore Social Welfare Deparment, I was called upon to mediate in a Tamil domestic dispute. A caring father and his hard-working teenage son were locked in a bitter misunderstanding over the young man's career plans. The son, with an excellent school record, hoped to apply to the Faculty of Engineering at the local university. The father did not realise that, by that point in time, this could lead to good career prospects. The son quoted him as saying, "I have worked hard with dirty hands so that you can take up a career with clean hands, and now you tell me that you want to be an engineer!" Regrettably, because of my linguistic limitations, I could only address their needs through the English-educated son.

This family lived at the back of the father's small suburban eating shop, which was run by the father and two paid assistants. At the family meeting at the Welfare Department, my attempts to focus on the needs of the father and the son were constantly impeded by the mother's loudly voiced and apparently endless complaints. Lamentably dependent on the interpreter, I could glean only that she was generally a person in loggerheads mode and was, most especially, in constant conflict with the father. She felt deeply frustrated at his refusal to allow her to participate in the running of the shop. She felt capable of managing the cash desk rather than just sitting around, bored to her wits' end, in the back room.

With so many rough labourers as patrons, how could her husband expose her to such contacts and would not his entire community mock him for being unable to support and protect his wife properly? I could empathise with the father's sense of standing in his community but this tall, masterful, middle-aged woman was undoubtedly capable of felling, with a single withering glance, any eating-shop patron unwise enough to speak or step out of turn.

In an attempt to clear the air of this storm of negative energy, I turned to the son and said, "Please ask your mother if she has memories of any time when she was truly happy." As things turned out, this was not a wise move on my part! In her immediate answer the lady, tall already, pulled herself to an even greater height, and glared at me with a look fierce enough to bleach hair. "Yes," said the son, clearly embarrassed, "she was very happy in the Indian National Army." Singapore was still a colony and my personal (English) appearance an unwitting but unfortunate reminder of this: I had opened the way for a final anti-imperialist salvo fired by the indomitable Rani of Jhansi regiment.

As I had been a fairly consistent reader of serious British newspapers since the early 1940s, it says something for the British need to blot out a painful memory that, until that day in 1956, I had never heard of the INA. It was some years before I was able to make good this omission in my knowledge of wartime affairs and to learn that India also had sought to airbrush from national memory the exploits of the INA. But the memory of that able, frustrated woman, wasting her talents in idleness in the back quarters of a shop always remained with me.

Like the "ranis" back on the rubber estates she was enduring the post-war fate of women, repeated in history. British women after World War I and still, if to a lesser extent after World War II, were also expected to step back from the unprecedented responsibilities they had taken on while the men were away. Indeed, while "the Colonel" was away in the Confederate Army (in the American Civil War), even the "Southern Belle" had proved she could run the plantation with great efficiency—somewhat to the dismay of said Colonel, returning from war and expecting the domestic authority pattern to be at status quo ante bellum. It can never be.

15

A Vignette of Violence

In Singapore of the early 1950s, violence reared its ugly head principally from two quite disparate directions.

First, there were the long established Chinese secret societies (SS), which thrived on "protection money" paid under threat of violence by those too afraid to resist these illegal demands (Mak 1981 provides, in eminently readable form, the complex role of secret societies in early Singapore). The most vulnerable to the SS demands were those engaged in marginally illegal activities, for example the organisers of prostitution, prostitutes themselves and professional gamblers. But many respectable shopkeepers and private medical practitioners (including an acquaintance of mine) found it easier to pay protection money demanded by whichever SS dominated the neighbourhood. At that time, the police was seen as quite unable to provide the protection which we would now expect as our right.

In 1958, the colonial government, preparing for a general election related to partial independence for Singapore, discovered that the SS were approaching politicians and offering to "sell" constituency votes. There was no way this criminal activity could be tackled by an open legal system, as witness intimidation was a well-known SS tactic. It was in this situation that a law was introduced which allowed detention without open trial. In place of open trial, the cases were reviewed by a closed-door tribunal, which included members of the public and lawyers in private practice. The tribunal reviewed the SS arrests and could endorse the police action. If, however, the members felt the arrest was unwarranted, they would refer the case back to the police for further investigation. This was the only way in which SS activity could be controlled.

The second source of violence was from extremist activities linked to politics among young students. Following the revolution in China in 1949, euphoria about this development generated anti-colonial, mainly idealistic, political activism, in the Chinese-language secondary schools in Singapore and (then) Malaya. This activism had, unfortunately, a sinister and violent fringe.

It so happened that one afternoon in 1952, I was in proximity to both these sources of violence. Neither involved any personal danger to myself, but both came close enough for me to gain a painful awareness of the horror involved.

A very good friend of mine, Mrs IY, a recent immigrant from China, was an afternoon-session teacher at the then Kim Yam Road branch of Chung Cheng High School. Because her family had been Roman Catholic for several generations they had decided to leave China in 1949, when the Communist government took over the country, as they feared there would be persecution of Christians. In China, Mrs IY had taught at a tertiary-level commercial college for young adults; in Singapore, her best option was a Chinese-language secondary school.

We had first met because I had answered an advertisement she had placed in the *Straits Times*, offering lessons in Cantonese language in return for English lessons. We had soon become such good friends that the formal teaching was forgotten! I am sure we both benefited linguistically from our time together, but this derived from our personal interaction rather than from any lessons.

On the day in question we had lunch together, during which my friend confided to me her state of near-panic-level fear. Without any warning or introduction, the day before, two new pupils appeared in her class of fifteen- and sixteen-year-old boys. Were these new pupils? Hardly! Mrs IY recognised the "new boys" as men aged twenty-four or twenty-five from her commercial class in China, masquerading as schoolboys. The only possible explanation was that they were political agents infiltrating the school system to strengthen the Communist component in student activism (see Lee 1998 for positive and negative aspects of Chinese school student activism). Mrs IY was in a state of terror lest they realised that she had recognised them, and was therefore a threat to their "cover".

Mrs IY feared for her life with good reason. In Penang the distinguished principal of a leading Chinese high school had been shot dead, following his open disagreement with his students' Communist agenda. In Singapore, the actively Christian (and therefore anti-Communist) principal of a Chinese-language girls' school had had a pail of acid thrown in her face. Her injuries were so severe that she had had to be sent abroad for skin-graft treatment to reduce the ghastly disfigurement she had suffered.

After lunch Mrs IY was planning to hand in her resignation with immediate effect. She felt that for her safety she must leave not just this school but the school system altogether, as the same situation might well arise elsewhere at any time. It was in a depressed and anxious state of mind that we drove up Kim Yam Road to her school that afternoon. In those days Kim Yam Road was not a very cheerful place at the best of times. Boys who walked up to the school never carried either cash or watches as the SS were dominant there and carried out petty robberies with impunity.

When I turned the car around at the school gate to return down to River Valley Road, I found I was in a queue. Cars were moving very slowly, and I could see that drivers were swerving to avoid some obstacle. When I finally came in view of the obstruction, I saw, to my horror, that it was the dead body of a young man, his neck slashed open. The blood had apparently congealed on the surface of the hot road—it was not running from his head but looked like a lump of liver. He was dressed all in black, and near his outstretched arm was a large *parang* (machete or cleaver). Clearly this was no innocent victim, but someone else's parang had got at him first.

It is hard to forget this tragic waste of life. Given other opportunities at an early age, he could have been a decent and useful young family man.

On a more positive note, the old "slum" houses on Kim Yam Road have been restored and it is an attractive, rather gentrified residential area. There is no longer any trace of a school having existed there. Mrs IY went on to make a successful career for herself in the travel business, and became a valued food editor of a Chinese-language newspaper. We remained lifelong friends, until her passing some years ago.

16

A Funeral in the Tan Family

"[S]ome malignant spell broods over the most solemn ceremonials and inserts into them some feature which makes them ridiculous ... Something always breaks down, somebody contrives to escape doing his part ... and ruin[s] it all" (Hobsbaum and Ranger 1983: 101). These are the words of Robert Arthur Talbot Gascoyne-Cecil—3rd Marquess of Salisbury who was the British prime minister from June 1865 to April 1868—but could apply perfectly to the account of a traditional Chinese funeral conducted in Singapore in 1953.

Mrs Emily Tan, a Methodist and educated at the Methodist Girls' School, was a feisty and "true-blue" Teochew Peranakan or Straits-born woman, who, like other such ladies of her generation, wore sarong with kebaya (voile jacket) as her everyday style of dress. It was my privilege to be present when Mrs Tan was regaling a group of her friends with the details of the recent funeral of her Peranakan mother-in-law, who had lived to over the age of ninety. Much loved and respected, the old lady had been frail and in a coma for several years, so the family was as much relieved as grieved at her passing. She had been a widow for several decades, secure and comfortably provided for by way of the business that her China-born husband had established and left behind.

At the time we spoke, this business was managed by Mrs Tan's husband, his only brother and the husband of one of the several sisters in the family. By the time of the matriarch's death, everyone was around or over sixty years of age. The two brothers were responsible for all the arrangements and expenses connected with their mother's funeral.

To Mrs Tan's extreme indignation, one of the sisters had reminded them that the old man had gone back to China to purchase the status of Mandarin, which meant that her mother-in-law's body should be dressed "in twenty-two layers of grave clothes". "Okay for her," snorted Mrs Tan. "She's not paying." Conveniently, the second brother then recalled that their father had had a wife in a village in China before he migrated to Singapore. The master of ceremonies (MC) provided by the funeral company assured them that, as a second wife, their mother was entitled only to eleven layers of grave clothes. In cases where a man had had a village wife in China, the wife in Singapore was usually regarded as a co-first wife (see Freedman 1958). But in this instance, it suited the family to downgrade the deceased lady to the status of second wife.

A man employed by the funeral company stood with arms outstretched while the thin, stiff, gauze open jackets were put on him—eleven layers, one at a time. The layers were then removed in one piece to be gently eased onto the body of the old lady. "Ugh, I didn't look," shuddered Mrs Tan, responding squeamishly as a Methodist to these "pagan" practices.

Finally, all the kin gathered for the ceremony of placing the body inside a huge, hollowed, appropriately carved tree trunk, which was the traditional coffin of those days. At this point the MC dictated that custom required the eldest daughter-in-law to place a pearl in the mouth of the corpse. In relating this, Mrs Tan pulled up to her full height. "I stood my ground. 'I'm a Christian,' I said. 'We don't do that kind of thing.'" At this point, the second daughter-in-law got cold feet. "She began whimpering and wriggling, and finally ran out to the back in a flood of tears."

An awkward silence followed and the assembled family began to get restive. Finally, a young man named Arthur, who was engaged to one of the granddaughters, stepped forward, bristling with impatience, and shouted, "Give me the bl***y pearl, I'll do it!" So it got done. "Aiyoh!" sighed Mrs Tan, recalling the undignified moment, but also the general relief all round.

A traditional Chinese funeral procession is supposed to set out at noon, when the sun is at its brightest and the harmful demons are assumed to lose their power. But the departure is notoriously always late—getting everyone organised can be difficult. Being modern and managerial in style, Mrs Tan determined that this was one funeral that would set out bang on time. She coaxed and supervised and generally "bossied about" (her phrase) and lo, the procession was ready to set out on the dot of noon—complete with the hearse, cars, the bus for mourners who did not have a car, and the funeral company's lorry with the wreaths. This was truly an achievement.

At this point, Mrs Tan smiled at us sheepishly and put her hand to her lips, embarrassed at recollecting her own naivety. The quite considerable procession, all prepared for the solemn ceremonials of committal, was right on time at the cemetery. Never in the history of that cemetery had a funeral procession ever arrived on time. To describe the state of the grave-diggers as flabbergasted would be an understatement—indeed, they were traumatised. Mrs Tan had omitted to "bossy" the grave-diggers, and the grave was not even half-ready. "There we were," she recalled with a sigh, "the living and the dead, all together under the shade of the trees, with nothing to do but just to wait. Aiyoh."

The Marquess of Salisbury would have nodded his wise and bearded head—he would have quite understood. His words, which he uttered in London around 1860 with reference to British ceremonial occasions, had indeed spanned time and space, making a great cross-cultural leap to 1953 Singapore while retaining the full essence of their original wisdom. Aiyoh indeed!

17

A Short Meditation on the Subject of
Wisdom

When some elderly person claims that by virtue of his being old he has wisdom to share, run for cover. He is more or less guaranteed to be on the verge of bombarding you with his opinions which, by virtue of his immodest claim, one can be almost certain will be a collection of personal biases and prejudice.

I say "he" for I have seen this more often in older men. But what of the occasional older woman with this self-delusion? Watch out, she has the Queen Bee syndrome, and the rest of us in that hive had better stop buzzing around and listen. As we will never get a word in edgeways we do not have much choice, unless we can manage to quietly sidle out and get on with our nectar collecting, or whatever. As the biology textbook says of the poisonous spider, "Of this species, the female is more deadly than the male."

It was close encounters with several self-proclaimed wise elders (who really were not), that set me thinking more seriously about what we mean by wisdom. It is, most certainly, not a built-in outcome of the process of aging although it is true that the longer you live, the more opportunities you have of acquiring wisdom: but only, and I repeat, only if you have made appropriate use of those opportunities. Wisdom, which is not the same as knowledge, may be more easily acquired during the social interaction involved in the acquiring of knowledge, but this does not necessarily happen for every individual.

Wisdom may encapsulate the idea of possessing good judgement in deciding how a situation should be handled. It seems that wisdom is intrinsically associated with the understanding and facilitating of interpersonal relationships which constitute, after all, the warp and woof of daily life.

During the course of a long life, one is witness to changes in how people deal with each other. If one is alert to this, one can make note of examples where someone has shown notable ability in handling a situation or series of situations in a manner that led to socially positive outcomes. And where someone has articulated this with insight, one can "catch" some of their wisdom. The best way I can explain this is by sharing some of my own experience that set me thinking on the subject of wisdom.

One of my outstanding memories dates from 1947, when I was twenty-one. I was registered as a graduate student at the University of London, and supplemented my resources by doing an occasional week of relief teaching in primary schools. At one school, I was called on several times when they were, for some reason or other, short-handed, and got to know the staff, and to admire the style of the headmaster, a Mr Butler. He had the ability of relating to the pupils in a friendly and informal manner while ensuring total conformity if discipline showed signs of getting out of hand. Because of its catchment area, there was more than an average number of hard-to-manage boys in that school.

On one occasion, Mr Butler sent for Benny, one of the most difficult boys in my class of eleven- and twelve-year-olds, and asked him to tidy his personal cupboard. In my naive twenty-one-year-old ignorance, I was indignant that this obvious privilege was not given as a reward to one of the more well-behaved boys in my class. When we met during the coffee-break, I chided Mr Butler for his choice of boy for this task. His answer has remained with me through all these years. "It is so hard to find anything to praise Benny for, that you have to invent something." It took me some time to digest the full meaning of this, but I came to realise that this was an example of true wisdom.

Punishment for our bad behaviour may teach us what not to do but we truly grow from our sense of achievement, from the self-esteem that comes from a positive outcome of our efforts. Mr Butler sought to give Benny an opportunity to feel the positivity that was the reward for acceptable behaviour. Why does the Singapore prison service invest so much in providing educational opportunities for inmates? Because the man who leaves prison with decent A-levels (or some other qualification) can look to a future more rewarding than would come from committing further crimes. Like Mr Butler, the policy makers in the prison service know that they have to invent opportunities for positive achievement.

One never can tell when an example of wisdom will "get up and hit you between the eyes", nor is wisdom necessarily associated with age. I recall an instance from around 1960, when I asked a nine-year-old from a Singapore school to name her favourite teacher. She promptly replied, "Mrs Gee." I was most surprised for I had taught in that school and recalled Mrs Gee loudly berating her class; in those days of non-air-conditioned classrooms, everyone's teaching style was public knowledge. I had incorrectly assumed that Mrs Gee was too tough to be popular with her class. "Why do you like Mrs Gee?" I asked the girl. "Because she is strict and jolly," came the immediate reply. Apparently, because Mrs Gee was confident that she could comfortably exercise control when necessary, she could be relaxed with her class at times, and even share jokes with them.

In the vocabulary of childhood, this nine-year old recognised the basic characteristics of all good human resource management.

Our sense of well-being requires a confidence that rules will be kept. A manager who is a pushover does not have happy workers, as they never know who will manage to get away with breaking rules that the rest feel bound to observe, which creates general insecurity. But an overly strict manager, who is generally dour and po-faced, is unlikely to be managing a workforce with high morale. "Strict and jolly" is a pretty good formula in any managerial setting.

Perhaps this is even more desirable than we have realised. Recent developments in psycho-neurology indicate that a manager who is always critical and tends to scold people can negatively affect even the physical health of the workforce. Tests have shown a marked rise in blood pressure amongst workers whose best efforts fail to receive the recognition and appreciation they feel they have earned (Goleman 2005 is a fascinating read on the physical health outcomes of different patterns of social interaction).

When the work situation is in the range of "strict and jolly", there are found to be positive health outcomes. Indeed as the popular saying goes, "Out of the mouths of babes ..."

Conclusion

Settling down to write a book of reminiscences is, in some ways, like planting a seedling that grows into a tree. One has a rough idea of the final shape of the full-grown tree, but cannot predict all the directions in which new branches will sprout.

The initial "seedling" of the present volume was to be no more than the placing on record of details of my Singapore experience which have been omitted from formal history books. This seemed an urgent task, as these details could easily be lost forever once they were no longer part of the memory of the living.

The rich ethnographies accumulated in the 1950s and 1960s by the students of the Social Studies Department of the then University of Malaya are a case in point. These treasures survive only in digital form, virtually retrievable only by the most determined postgraduate scholar, and some indeed have been lost. It seemed to me important that all this interesting information about their own society should be available not only to the academic elite, but also to average citizens with secondary education.

I sought also to get on record some statistically significant but unpublished data on Tiger Year women. It had always worried me that the late great demographer Dr Tye Cho Yook had never published his rich data on how families of an earlier period had solved the problems of arranging a marriage for a daughter born in the Year of the Tiger. I pressed him to publish off and on, but it never happened. Thinking about all this, I wrote Chapter 1, which includes the revelation of my own lamentable Tiger horoscope.

This sparked in my mind thoughts about my personal experience of sixty-six years in a cultural setting quite different from that into which I was born and brought up. I also started thinking about how I had initially benefited from culture learning in my own society, before I ever ventured across the world into a completely new social setting. The best way to recommend this mode of learning at home to Singaporean readers was to include my personal "adventure", so out popped Chapter 2 with shades of *Downton Abbey*.

I have found, among friends and acquaintances, a tendency to assume that problems in Singapore were uniquely colonial, and that everything was managed with near perfection in the home country of the metropolitan power. This is so far from the truth that I wanted to clear the air on this. For example, prior to the post-World War II move towards a welfare state, there had been much truly grinding poverty in Britain, and cash assistance was handed out only on the most stringent means testing. And formal healthcare was, for the most part, out of reach of the poor.

To include all this in the present volume was too major a task. But the fact that much of Britain, like Singapore, lacked modern sanitation, well illustrated the fact that problems were not a colonial monopoly. I discuss this in Chapter 11.

The original plan was to keep the focus firmly on Singapore, with references to myself only where my experience provided some useful illustration. However, the publishers thought otherwise and insisted on the inclusion of Chapter 5, which is a very personal account of the years I spent learning the culture in Singapore. This chapter was considered necessary to document how I came to have any Singapore reminiscences to write about. My culture learning took a great leap forward as soon as I joined the staff of the Methodist Girls' School. Therefore, it seemed essential to refer to the rejoicing about a forthcoming staff marriage, which was the centre of conversation at the time I arrived in the staffroom as the new teacher. The history behind this marriage proved to be so detailed and dramatic that it could not just slip into the learning I gained from my time at MGS and merited a chapter all to itself. Hence Chapter 6 which records the tragic impact of war on one Johor family.

A major problem in assembling a book of oral memories is deciding when to close shop! Social encounters so often add one more new insight into the past. After having sent the initial draft of the early chapters to my publisher, an acquaintance told me about the marriage of a Tiger woman of my generation to a cousin with a tarnished reputation, as a last resort. And from another acquaintance came an anecdote about another such Tiger lady whose family had accepted a suitor from a family of much lower status than they would normally have regarded as an eligible match. Gems which were too late to be included in this volume!

The subject matter of Chapter 12, which discusses the problems of naming, is perhaps the most challenging for a firm closure to this volume—it seems as if everyone over the age of fifty knows of a problem arising from the brush of illiteracy with bureaucracy. The unfortunate gentleman who is named … bin Apa when his brothers are all … bin Osman only came to my notice as late as June 2016.

I can only hope that the final outcome will seem to my dear editor friends—whom I have thanked in the Acknowledgements—to have justified their input.

Bibliography

Baginda, Abdullah Malim. "The Boyanese (Baweanese) of Singapore", academic exercise. Singapore Department of Social Studies, University of Malaya, 1959. Microform.

Chang Soo. "Chinese Lineage Settlements in Singapore", academic exercise. Singapore: Department of Social Studies, University of Malaya, 1960.

Ch'en Ta. *Emigrant Communities in South China: A Study of Overseas Migration and its Influence on Standards of Living and Social Change.* New York: Institute of Pacific Relations, 1940.

Chia Cheong Fook. "The Place of the Hawker in the Community", academic exercise. Singapore: Department of Social Studies University of Malaya, 1954. Microform.

Chua, Albert. "Small States at the United Nations". In *50 Years of Singapore and the United Nations*, ed. Tommy Koh, Li Lin Chang and Joanna Koh, pp. 45–50. Singapore: World Scientific, 2015.

Corner, E.J.H. *The Marquis: A Tale of Syonan-to.* Singapore: Heinemann Asia, 1981.

Dhillon, Gurbaksh Singh. *From My Bones: Memoirs of Col. Gurbaksh Singh Dhillon.* New Delhi: Aryan Books International, 1998.

Flanders, Judith. *Inside the Victorian Home: A Portrait of Domestic Life in Victorian England.* New York and London: W.W. Norton, 2004.

Freedman, Maurice. *Chinese Family and Marriage in Singapore.* London: Her Majesty's Stationery Office, 1957.

___. *Chinese Lineage and Society: Fukien and Kwangtung.* London: Athlone Press (1966) 1971.

Goh, Keng Swee. *Urban Incomes & Housing: A Report on the Social Survey of Singapore, 1953–54.* Singapore: Government Printing Office, 1958.

Goh, Soon Phing. *Some Aspects of Women's Life in a Singapore Chinese Fishing Village: With Special References to Childcare and Pregnancy Beliefs and Practices in the Village.* Singapore: Department of Social Studies, University of Malaya, 1955.

Goleman, Daniel. *Social Intelligence: The New Science of Human Relationships.* New York: Bantam Books, 2006.

Handy, Ellice. *Eastern Exotica: Featuring Recipes.* Singapore: MPH Magazines, 1978.

___. *My Favourite Recipes.* Singapore: MPH Pub., 1990.

Hobsbaum, Eric and Terence Ranger (ed.). *The Invention of Tradition.* New York: Cambridge University Press, 1983.

Jackson, Robert Nicholas. *Pickering: Protector of Chinese.* Kuala Lumpur, Oxford and London: Oxford University Press, 1965.

Kaur, Manmohan. *Women in India's Freedom Struggle*, 3rd ed. New Delhi: Sterling (1985) 1992.

Kaye, Barrington. *Upper Nankin Street: A Sociological Study of Chinese Households Living in a Densely Populated Area.* Singapore: University of Malaya Press, 1960.

Kellmer Pringle, Mia, Neville Roy Butler and Ronald Davie. *11,000 Seven-Year-Olds: First Report of the National Child Development Study (1958 Cohort) Submitted to the Central Advisory Council (England) April 1966.* London: Longmans, 1966.

Kenneison, Rebecca. *Playing for Malaya: A Eurasian Family in the Pacific War.* Singapore: NUS Press, 2012.

Lau Fong, Mak. *The Sociology of Secret Societies. A Study of Chinese*

Secret Societies in Singapore and Peninsula Malaysia. Kuala Lumpur and New York: Oxford University Press, 1981.

Lebra, Joyce C. *Women against the Raj: the Rani of Jhansi Regiment*. Singapore: Institute of Southeast Asian Studies, 2008.

Lee, Edwin. *Historic Buildings in Singapore*. Singapore: Preservation of Monuments Board, 1990.

Lim, Patricia Pui Huen. "War and Ambivalence". In *War and Memory in Malaysia and Singapore*, ed. Patricia Pui Huen Lim and Diana Wong. Singapore: Institute of Southeast Asian Studies, 2008.

Lip, Evelyn. *Fun with Chinese Horoscopes*. Singapore: Graham Brash, 1987.

Manderson, Lenore. *Sickness and the State: Health and Illness in Colonial Malaya, 1870–1940*. Cambridge and New York: Cambridge University Press, 1996.

McNair, John Frederick Adolphus and W.D. Bayliss. *Prisoners their Own Warders*. Westminster: A. Constable, 1899.

Shinozaki, Mamoru. *My Wartime Experiences in Singapore*. Singapore: Institute of Southeast Asian Studies, 1973.

Singapore Children's Society. *Speaking of Children: The Singapore Children's Society Collected Lectures*. Singapore: World Scientific, 2016.

Stockard, J.E. *Daughters of the Canton Delta: Marriage Patterns and Economic Strategies in South China, 1860–1930*. Stanford, CA: Stanford University Press, 1989.

Stokes, Charles J. "A Theory of Slums", *Land Economics*, 38, 3 (August 1962): 187–97.

Tan, Francis. "Teochew Kongsi Houses in Singapore", academic exercise. Singapore: Department of Social Work and Social Administration, University of Singapore, 1963.

Tan, Karen. "World Toilet Day". In *50 Years of Singapore and the United Nations*, ed. Tommy Koh, Li Lin Chang and Joanna Koh, pp. 51–7. Singapore: World Scientific, 2015.

Toye, Hugh. *The Springing Tiger: A Study of a Revolutionary*. London: Cassell, 1959.

Vaughan, J.D. *The Manners and Customs of the Chinese of the Straits Settlements*. Kuala Lumpur: Oxford University Press (1879) 1971.

Warren, James Francis. *Ah Ku and Karayuki-san: Prostitution in Singapore, 1870-1940*. Singapore and New York: Oxford University Press, 1993.

Warren, Max. *Perspective in Mission*. London: Hodder and Stoughton, 1964.

Wee, Ann Elizabeth. "Some Social Implications of Rehousing Programmes in Singapore". In *The City as a Centre of Change in Asia*, ed. D.J. Dwyer. Hong Kong: Hong Kong University Press, 1972.

___. "Chinese Daughters of Indian Parents". In *Community Problems and Social Work in Southeast Asia*, ed. Peter Hodge. Hong Kong: Hong Kong University Press, 1980.

___. "Older Women from Colonial Times to the Present Day". In *Singapore Women: Three Decades of Change*, ed. Aline K. Wong and Leong Wai Kum. Singapore: Times Academic Press, 1993.

___. "The Way We Were: The Singapore Family of Times Past". In *The Ties that Bind*. AWARE Publication. Singapore: Armour Publishing, 1996.

___. "The Fellow-villager Dormitory and the Single Chinese Immigrant". In *Ethnic Chinese at the Turn of the Centuries*, ed. Zhuang Guotu. Xiamen: Xiamen University, 1997.

___. "Children and Childhood in the Singapore Chinese Family: Some Observations over Five Decades". In *Speaking of Children: The Singapore Children's Society Collected Lectures*, ed. Singapore Children's Society. New Jersey: World Scientific, 2016.

Wright, Lawrence. *Clean and Decent. The Fascinating History of the Bathroom & the Water Closet, and of Sundry Habits, Fashions & Accessories of the Toilet, Principally in Great Britain, France, & America*. New York: Viking Press, 1960.

Yang, C.K. *Chinese Communist Society: The Family and the Village.* Cambridge, MA: MIT Press (1959) 1965.